The Birds *of* Den Rock Park

Lawrence and Andover, Massachusetts

*A **Guide** to the **History** and **Natural History** of **Den Rock Park** and its **Birds***

By SUSAN HEGARTY

With a Summary of the Archaeology and Native History of Den Rock by EDWARD L. BELL

Mass Nature
Andover, Massachusetts

To Mary, Happy Birthday! Love, Susan

Copyright © 2013 by Susan Hegarty.
All rights reserved.

Published by: Mass Nature, P.O. Box 5073, Andover, MA 01810
www.massnature.com

ISBN: 978-0-9884456-0-4

First Edition

Printed in the United States of America

Photos by the author unless otherwise noted.

Front Cover: Red-Winged Blackbird singing from Den Rock Park's Beaver Pond
Back Cover: Downy Woodpecker on a cattail in the Beaver Pond.

Library of Congress Control Number: 2012919157

This paper meets the requirements of ANSI/ NISO Z39.48-1992
(Permanence of Paper)

Contents

INTRODUCTION..1

OVERVIEW OF THE PARK.............................2

HISTORY OF DEN ROCK PARK 4
    Archaeology and Native History of the Den Rock Area 4
    Recent History of Den Rock Park........................12

HABITATS 15
    Beaver Pond...15
    Oak Forest 16
    Shawsheen River 17

A CHANGING ENVIRONMENT......................... 18

THE BIRDS... 27
    Canada Goose 27
    Wood Duck 30
    Mallard 32
    Great Blue Heron 33
    Green Heron 36
    Black-crowned Night-Heron............................37
    Red-tailed Hawk 40
    Mourning Dove...42
    Belted Kingfisher.......................................45
    Red-bellied Woodpecker 46
    Downy Woodpecker....................................47
    Hairy Woodpecker 48
    Northern Flicker 50

Eastern Phoebe 51

Eastern Kingbird. 53

Blue Jay. 54

American Crow. 56

Tree Swallow 59

Black-capped Chickadee 61

Tufted Titmouse 62

White-breasted Nuthatch. 63

Eastern Bluebird 64

American Robin 66

European Starling 67

Song Sparrow. 71

Northern Cardinal 72

Red-winged Blackbird 74

Common Grackle 78

Brown-headed Cowbird. 82

House Sparrow 87

Appendix A: Bird and Mammal Species Extirpated from Massachusetts since the Beginning of the Colonial Period . . .89

Appendix B: List of Bird Species 94

Bibliography 97

Acknowledgments 114

Introduction

This guide provides information on 30 species of birds that occur in the Den Rock area. It includes permanent and seasonal residents that are commonly seen in the park, as well as some occasional visitors. The first part of the guide summarizes general and historical information about the park and its surrounding landscape, and provides descriptions of the park's habitats.

Den Rock Park has a long and fascinating history. The Native American history of Den Rock goes back thousands of years and is described in a section of this guide written by archaeologist Edward L. Bell.

During the past few hundred years, the local landscape has changed dramatically as a result of European settlement, land development, and industrialization. Many of the bird species found at Den Rock have been heavily impacted by human activities. This guide includes a section that describes the historic changes that have taken place in the region and the subsequent effects on birds, as well as an overview of current and future threats to birds. The individual species accounts in the latter part of the guide include information on food and nesting habitats, historical occurrences and abundances, and other information of local relevance.

A Canada Goose in Den Rock's Beaver Pond. March 12, 2011.

Overview of the Park

The Den Rock Park conservation area occupies approximately 130 acres in Lawrence and Andover, Massachusetts. It consists of a forested 80-acre park in Lawrence (owned by the City of Lawrence), and approximately 50 acres of adjacent conservation land in Lawrence and Andover (owned by the Merrimack River Watershed Council and the City of Lawrence). Technically the park includes only the 80-acre parcel in Lawrence; however, the combined 130-acre conservation area is commonly referred to as "Den Rock Park."

The rock outcrop at Den Rock Park.

The park is named for an approximately 30-foot tall granite outcrop, situated in the eastern portion of the property. Over four miles of hiking trails wind through the park, leading to the rock outcrop, the Shawsheen River, and a large beaver pond.

Den Rock Park is considered an "urban wilderness." It is an area of natural habitat surrounded by development, including Route 114, Interstate 495, an active railroad line, two large apartment complexes, Stirling Street and associated residences. It is the largest park in Lawrence and one of the few remaining natural areas in the city. The portion of the park owned by the City of Lawrence is managed and maintained by the City of Lawrence and by Groundwork Lawrence in

View of the Beaver Pond from an outlook on the northern edge of the pond.

partnership with the Massachusetts Audubon Society. Recreational uses of the park include walking/hiking, rock climbing, and birding.

The main entrance is located off of Route 114 in Lawrence. The park may also be accessed from a trailhead off of Stirling Street in Andover.

Den Rock Park. MassGIS 2001 half meter color orthophoto.

History of Den Rock Park

Archaeology and Native History of the Den Rock Area

By Edward L. Bell
Senior Archaeologist
Massachusetts Historical Commission, Boston

Ancient Native Americans arrived in the Shawsheen River drainage about 12,600 years ago. Ancient Native groups maintained and fostered contacts and connections throughout eastern North America. Inventive technologies and creative lifeways were part of Native traditions that lasted for millennia. Some traditions such as diet, cooking methods, storage technologies, tool forms and burial practices were similar on a subcontinental scale. Native traditions, even everyday activities were imbued with ceremonies of thanksgiving, an ethic of sharing and receiving, and expectations of sustainability and continuance. These were a people cognizant of their own deep history, and socially connected to their familiar, established places recurrently occupied for thousands upon thousands of years. Through language, manners, ritual, art, dress, foodways and technology these ancient people expressed their individualities, their belonging and obligations with relatives, acquaintances, and ancestors, and their relationships to other groups in other places near and far.

Native American archaeological sites are rare because many were located in some of the first areas to be occupied by the colonists, long since developed as cities and suburbs. The few remaining and intact archaeological sites in Massachusetts are located on conserved and undeveloped land. Archaeological studies of ancient Native American cultures focus on a limited range of objects and places that preserve rare evidence of their activities and creative traditions. New England's acidic soils do not preserve the whole range of ancient objects created from wood, plant and animal parts. Typically, only stone, pottery, metal, burned bone and seeds, and firewood charcoal survive.

The first archaeological discoveries in Den Rock Park were casual finds, but there is no record of the exact discovery locations within the park. Before 1901 Mr. and Mrs. F. E. Hibbard collected two stone tools from Den Rock, one described as an "axe" and the other confusingly called an "adz-gouge." The latter object is in the Robert S. Peabody Museum of Archaeology. A pecked groove around the stone is where it was hafted in a wooden handle; its rounded ends show it was not an adze or a gouge, but was a pounding stone that could be used to drive stakes, to flatten wood for baskets or mats, to crush rock in pottery-making, and for other handy purposes (Figure 1).

Figure 1. Hafted Pounding Stone. Robert S. Peabody Museum of Archaeology Accession No. 59244. Photo by Edward L. Bell.

Sometime in the early to mid-20th century, James Wallace Smith, a local avocational archaeologist, excavated two areas of Den Rock Park. The few records and artifacts saved from Smith's dig indicate that he located evidence of established Native occupation in the Den Rock area. Fragments of a steatite (soapstone) cooking pot dating around 4,000 to 3,700 years ago (2050 B.C. to 1750 B.C.) (Figure 2); a woman's pestle or hand-held pounding stone for processing food (Figure 3); and, a very small and broken chipped tool that resembles the tip of a drill, an awl or a projectile point (an arrow, dart or spear point) (Figure 4) are the only artifacts preserved from the dig. Smith's notes say he also found projectile points, knives, drills, hundreds of chips of rock from stone tool-making and an "effigy knife." Food preparation for feasts, stone tool production, and possibly basketry or building structures are among the activities that demonstrate creativity and proficiency learned and practiced through generations.

Figure 2. Steatite Cooking Pot Fragments, Interior View. Robert S. Peabody Museum of Archaeology Accession No. 90.72. Photo by Edward L. Bell.

Figure 3. Pestle or Pounding Stone, Length ca. 17.5 cm. Robert S. Peabody Museum of Archaeology Accession No. 90.72.

Because Smith did not produce a report of his investigation, and very few artifacts and only sketchy, undated records from his explorations are preserved, only partial information about those sites can be gleaned. Modern archaeological practices now require exacting field methods, record-keeping and reporting, and permanent preservation of complete archaeological collections. The area around Den Rock Park is now protected land. Archaeological sites are fragile and extremely vulnerable to irreparable damage from casual digging and artifact collecting. State and federal laws prohibit digging or artifact collecting to protect these ancient and historical places.

Figure 4. Black Rhyolite Biface Fragment, Perhaps a Drill, Awl, or Projectile Point. Robert S. Peabody Museum of Archaeology Accession No. 90.72. Photo by Edward L. Bell.

Development of land for new construction also endangers ancient and historic sites. Proposed projects that involve federal, state and some local government agencies undergo review and professional study to ascertain if important historic and archaeological resources will be affected. Before a housing complex was constructed near Den Rock Park in the late 1990s, professional archaeologists systematically tested the areas planned for development. Careful excavation, precise record-keeping, laboratory work, research and writing went into the discovery and understanding of the archaeological sites. Archaeologists identified seven areas that had evidence of ancient and historical period Native American activities.

Six of the archaeological sites found during the survey in the 1990s were short-term campsites and working areas used by few individuals in passing, or overnight to a few weeks. Activities around these established sites included hunting animals for food; gathering plants for food and medicine, and possibly for weaving mats and baskets; manufacturing and sharpening stone tools; and cooking and eating. Although archaeologists found nothing to precisely date these six sites, comparative information suggests that they likely date from about 5,000 to 500 years ago. The Shawsheen River nearby was a watercraft route, and wetlands in this area supported many animals and plants. Native people were attracted to this location for its favorable resources and sheltering landscape. Den Rock, with its dramatic exposed cliffs, sheared slabs and boulders of sparkling biotite granitic gneiss, was an ancient landmark.

The most important archaeological site discovered was sequently occupied by Native Americans, at least between the 1st and 3rd centuries, between the 6th to 9th centuries, between the 13th to 15th centuries, and in the 17th century. (Accurate and precise data to date the site occupations are limited. The occupational history is undoubtedly more complex and prolonged.) The location was used for creating ceramic cooking and storage vessels and clay tobacco pipes, for fashioning stone tools, as a base for gathering and hunting forays, for food preparation and cooking, and for many other everyday activities.

Artifacts included thousands of pieces of finished and unfinished Native American pottery vessels and a few fragments of tobacco pipes; burned animal bone and charcoal; several kinds of flint tools including possible gunflints, fire-starter "strike-a-lights," and other tools made using English flint; and stone tool manufacturing waste of several kinds of rock. The clay for the pottery and some of the local stone was obtained immediately nearby. Volcanic rock types came from places within a day's travel. The English flint was from the coast where English ships had offloaded ballast rock. Good tool-making rock could be obtained through relatives and acquaintances.

Interestingly, Native tool-makers used English flint to fashion traditional Native stone tools such as a drill, an engraving tool, scrapers for working leather, bone, wood, bark, or reedy plants, and an arrowhead. The gunflints and strike-a-lights were made in Native ways. Other artifacts included a fragment of sheet copper (probably an unfinished tool being made from a European cooking pot), several pieces of a 17th-century glass bottle, and a metal gun part from a 17th-century snaphaunce-type firearm.
Even in the mid- to late 17th century, decades after English colonists were living in their homelands, Native people maintained their traditions of stone tool and pottery-making, incorporated some new and interesting European materials in traditionally inventive and adaptive Native ways, and continued to occupy a Native place familiar to them and to hundreds of generations of their ancestors. The Den Rock area was eventually a refuge for Native people from the disruptive and dislocating presence of the English colonists in their homelands.

The Native residents of the Essex County area who first observed English explorers and colonists in their homelands were part of the Penacook-Pawtucket and Massachusett groups, and one local group was sometimes called Naumkeag. The history of the 16th and 17th-century Native residents is incompletely known. The written information that survives from the early historical period was inaccurately and incompletely recorded by Europeans who did not fully understand and appreciate the diversity, complexity and relationships of Native people and their cultures. Sweeping epidemics from European pathogens decimated about 90% of the New England Native population by the 1620s, leaving about 10,000 survivors, while the population of the English in New England grew from about 3,000 in 1630 to 33,000 in 1660.

The Den Rock area was part of Cochichawick (renamed Andover in 1646 from which Lawrence was established much later). A few English squatters may have arrived as early as 1634, when the Native population was estimated to be about 50 individuals. English settlement began in earnest about 1643. Negotiated agreements between Native leaders and English in 1644 and 1646 attempted to form alliances and to ensure that Native residents could continue to occupy and use the area for fishing and planting. Unceasing encroachment into Native homelands and dispossession of Native families from their properties and resources ineludibly led to social and economic duress, resistance, and conflict. After the war of 1675–1676, New England Native people endured and persisted as a distinctive presence.

Local history books mention the recollections of residents from the mid- to late 19th century about Native people making "pilgrimages" to Native cemeteries in Lawrence; and about Nancy Parker, a woman of Native ancestry who lived a few miles from Den Rock. In her later years Mrs. Parker spun yarn or thread for income; until recently, history books did not mention that she was once married to the Revolutionary War veteran Salem Poor who died in poverty in 1802. In 1876 and again in the early to mid-20th century, little hillocks were seen in Den Rock Park and thought to be the remnants of a Native woman's garden. The casual discovery of artifacts and rudimentary digs in the first half of the 20th century, the systematic excavations of the late 1990s, and writings and studies in the early 21st century all remind local residents of the Native history of the Den Rock area. Recounting the archaeology and history of Native places renews memories and connections of local people about familiar places. Native American people continue to reside in this area and have a deep interest in the history and preservation of their ancestral, historical, and cultural places.

For more information about Massachusetts archaeology, visit the websites of the Massachusetts Historical Commission, the Robert S. Peabody Museum of Archaeology, and the Massachusetts Archaeological Society. Please help to protect, preserve and appreciate ancient and historic places as heritage resources. Please remember that archaeological sites are rare, fragile and extremely vulnerable to irreparable damage from digging, artifact collecting, and land development. Please support statewide efforts to conserve the Commonwealth's non-renewable cultural resources for present and future generations.

Acknowledgments:

This interpretation is based on the results of the Den Rock area investigations, analyses, and writings by Jeffrey Robert Carovillano, Craig S. Chartier, Elena Décima, Martin G. Dudek, Michael Katherine Haynie, Eric S. Johnson, Tonya Baroody Largy, and Bruce M. Patterson. I am grateful to Susan Hegarty for prompting this writing, and for bringing the Hibbard and Smith collections to my attention, and to Bonnie K. Sousa who facilitated access to the collections at the Robert S. Peabody Museum of Archaeology. Anna Hayden, Dave Hill and Jonathan K. Patton assisted the editing and composition.

Recent History of Den Rock Park

According to Maurice Dorgan's *Lawrence, Yesterday and Today (1845-1918)*, the first non-native Americans to occupy the Den Rock site were members of a family named Peters, who operated a brick yard on the property. The Peters family owned the land until 1877 when it was purchased by the City of Lawrence for a cemetery. Although initial preparations were made, the Den Rock property was never used as a cemetery. Instead, the city's Park Commissioners took over the management of the land and contemplated turning it into a quarry. However, despite these considerations, in 1896 the 80-acre property was designated as a city park.

In 1935, improvements were made to the park property by workers under the Federal Emergency Relief Administration (FERA) program. FERA was created as part of President Roosevelt's New Deal to combat the Great Depression. It provided grants to states for public work projects to employ people who were out of work. In addition to building trails, "ERA" workmen constructed rock steps, "rustic walks" and "rustic fireplaces." The "rustic walks" were made of wood and were built around the base of the rock outcropping to make it easier for people to walk around the rock. The "rustic fireplaces" were made of stone. In addition to these features, two open air theaters were reportedly constructed in the park around that time.

During the late 1950s, Interstate 495 was built west of Den Rock Park. Some of the material used to construct the highway was taken from a sand and gravel pit located south of the park. The gravel pit reportedly remained in operation until 1963.

In 1995, land in Andover abutting the park was rezoned from industrial to residential. Shortly thereafter, a 16-acre residential subdivision was built south of the park on some of the land formerly used for sand and gravel operations. Other land located adjacent to the park in Andover and Lawrence that was not used for the development was donated to the Merrimack River Watershed Council. This land came to be informally considered part of Den Rock Park, expanding the size of the park to 130 acres.

During the past decade additional improvements were made to the park. In 2003, the Student Conservation Association built a pathway to the park from Stirling Street, and in 2004 and 2005, the City of Lawrence and Groundwork Lawrence oversaw the construction of a new visitor parking area at the Route 114 entrance, and performed various trail improvements.

∗∗

For much of its history, Den Rock Park was a subject of controversy and debate. Initially, there was controversy over whether the Den Rock property should be made into a park—even after it was designated as such. Although it was used as a recreational area by residents for decades, it was not finally made into a park until the 1930s, when trails were constructed and other features were added.

Yet for more than 60 years after the park was built, the City of Lawrence continued to struggle over whether to keep Den Rock as a park or let it be used for some other purpose that would financially benefit the city. Some members of local government were in favor of selling all or part of the park property to developers to gain tax revenues for the city. Proposed development plans for Den Rock reportedly included, among other things, an industrial park and a rubbish processing plant. In 1995, the park and adjacent parcels were proposed to be converted into a nine-hole golf course, mall and housing units. These proposals were strongly opposed by members of the community, who feared seeing the city's largest park destroyed.

Fortunately—thanks to the efforts of the park's many supporters over the years—no portion of the property was ever developed or sold. Among the park's advocates was Harold R. Rafton, for whom the Harold R. Rafton Reservation in Andover is now named. In 1962, Mr. Rafton was honored by the Massachusetts Audubon Society for having "led the fight which prevented the destruction of Den Rock Park in Lawrence in 1960–1961, by developers." Another supporter of the park was Oscar M. Root, a professor at the Brooks School in North Andover, who wrote *The Birds of the Andover Region* (1957–58), which was used as a resource in the writing of this guide.

In 2007, the City of Lawrence created a new zoning district for Den Rock Park to ensure that the park would remain undeveloped and preserved in a natural state for the foreseeable future. The new zoning, designated as "open space conservation" was established "to preserve natural resources and environmentally significant areas while promoting public access for passive recreation." Only infrastructure consistent with this zoning is allowed in the park (i.e., trails, educational signage, walkways, and public parking areas), with any new work subject to review and approval by the Lawrence Conservation Commission.

Habitats

Den Rock Park consists primarily of oak forest with wetlands occurring along the periphery. The Shawsheen River and associated wetlands are located in the western portion of the park. Wetlands also occur along the southern boundary, northwest of the Stirling Street trailhead (an area known as "The Marsh," which was part of the former sand and gravel pit); and along the eastern edge of the park, extending from Stirling Street to Route 114. The wetland/stream system in the eastern portion of the property is impacted by beavers. The southern portion of this area, which abuts Stirling Street, contains the most productive bird habitat in the park. This area is referred to as the "Beaver Pond" and is the focus of this guide. Other habitats of note in the park are the oak forest and the Shawsheen River.

Beaver Pond

The Beaver Pond may be viewed from Stirling Street in Andover or from an outlook located along the northern edge of the pond in Lawrence (accessible via Den Rock's trail system). It contains numerous logs and dead standing trees, which provide perches and nesting areas for a number of species. The pond is flooded throughout the year but experiences large decreases in water levels during the summer. Water in the Beaver Pond wetland system drains to the north, eventually discharging to the Shawsheen River north of Route 114. The northern section of Stirling Street (constructed in the early 2000s as part of the Stirling Woods residential development) crosses the western portion of the wetland system. A row of planted pine trees is located along the edge of Stirling Street, providing a buffer to the pond.

The Beaver Pond at Den Rock Park, as viewed from Stirling Street in Andover.

In the 1990s, the portion of this wetland in the vicinity of Den Rock Park and what is now Stirling Street, consisted of Red Maple Swamp. Water flowed through the swamp via intermittent streams, which consisted of shallow ditches that had been dug at some point in the past for drainage.

To mitigate for wetland impacts resulting from the Stirling Woods residential development, wetland replication areas were created adjacent to the existing wetland, expanding its boundaries in those areas. Subsequently, the wetland became flooded by beavers, resulting in the current beaver pond.

Fish and a number of amphibian and reptile species utilize this habitat, including Spring Peepers, Green Frogs, American Bullfrogs, Gray Tree Frogs, Painted Turtles, Snapping Turtles, and Garter Snakes. Beaver and Muskrat may be occasionally observed in the pond, and at times White-tailed Deer may be seen browsing along the edge. During March and April, various duck species are found in the pond, including Wood Duck and Hooded Merganser. Numerous ducks may also be seen during fall migration. Chickadees, woodpeckers, and other birds occur here year-round, and many other species of birds frequent the pond on a seasonal basis.

Oak Forest

The oak forest at Den Rock Park contains a large number of nut and berry-producing plants, which provide a rich food source to many animals. Acorns are consumed by various species of birds including Blue Jays, Wild Turkeys, White-breasted Nuthatches, Tufted Titmice, Common Grackles, Red-bellied Woodpeckers, Hairy Woodpeckers, Northern Flickers, Wood Ducks, and Mallards. In addition, oaks provide food to a huge diversity of insects, which in turn are eaten by birds. Oaks

The oak forest at Den Rock Park.

support more species of Lepidoptera (i.e., butterflies/moths), an important food for birds, than any other plant genus. In addition, cavities in oak trees provide nesting sites for species such as Black-capped Chickadees, Hairy Woodpeckers, Tufted Titmice, and White-breasted Nuthatches.

In addition to oaks, other abundant food-producing plants in the forest include blueberries, chokeberry, Black Huckleberry, Shagbark Hickory, American Hazelnut, and Maple-leaf Viburnum.

SHAWSHEEN RIVER

The Shawsheen River, located near the western boundary of Den Rock Park, originates in Bedford, near Hanscom Air Force Base. From there it flows northeast, winding through densely developed areas before discharging into the Merrimack River in Lawrence, north of Den Rock Park.

The Shawsheen River as viewed from Den Rock Park.

Water quality in the river has improved considerably since 1972, with the elimination of almost all industrial discharges and notable decreases in pollutants. In the vicinity of Den Rock Park, wildlife habitat associated with the river is somewhat compromised due to fragmentation by roads and noise from Interstate 495. However, the river provides open water habitat for ducks and geese during most of the year, including times when many other bodies of water are frozen. Songbirds, including Black-capped Chickadees, American Robins, American Goldfinches, and Dark-eyed Juncos are frequently seen foraging near the river. Recently, Fishers have also been observed in this area.

A Changing Environment

The environment surrounding Den Rock has undergone considerable change over the years. Prior to the arrival of European colonists, the interior of New England was mostly forested; during pre-colonial times, over 85 percent of Massachusetts was covered by forest. Initial widespread clearing of land occurred mostly during the 1700s as a result of European settlement.

In 1844, the land constituting what is now Lawrence (formerly parts of Andover and Methuen) was largely agricultural. Agricultural activity and deforestation reached a peak in Massachusetts during the mid- to late 1800s, during which time forest cover in the state reached its lowest level of approximately 20 percent. Most of the forest that remained consisted of wooded lots, which were heavily managed for firewood and timber.

Between 1845 and 1855 industrial development in Lawrence proceeded at a rapid pace, and much farmland was lost to buildings and other development. Agriculture began to decline throughout New England, as some farmers moved west in search of more productive land, while others pursued factory jobs in lieu of farming. Over time, abandoned farmland in New England once again became forested.

With the loss of farms, forest cover in Massachusetts increased to approximately 70 percent by the mid- to late 1900s, but has been declining since then as a result of development. Today approximately 60 percent of the land in Massachusetts is forested.

***

As you flip through this guide you will find that several species of birds that are currently very common in our area did not occur in this region at all 150 to 200 years ago. Some other species that we take for granted were nearly extirpated in the recent past and have made remarkable recoveries. Large-scale changes in forest cover and other factors, such as hunting, pesticide use, invasive species, and loss of habitat, have affected bird populations and distributions over the years, both locally and globally.

In the past, birds and other wildlife were hunted without restriction. Trees were cut down and wetlands were filled for agriculture on a massive scale, and pollutants were discharged into the environment without regulation. Such practices affected species throughout the state. The American Beaver was eliminated from the Massachusetts landscape by the late 1700s from intensive hunting, the loss of trees, and the draining of wetlands. Over-hunting claimed the last of the Wild Turkeys in the Commonwealth by the mid-1850s, and by 1910 our national symbol, the Bald Eagle, was eliminated due to deliberate shooting and loss of habitat. Several other species of birds and mammals were extirpated from Massachusetts (Appendix A).

Fortunately, in recent times attitudes and practices have changed for the better. The beaver, the Wild Turkey, and the Bald Eagle have since been reestablished in the state. Over the past 100 years, several pieces of legislation have been enacted to protect the environment including the Migratory Bird Treaty Act, the Clean Air Act, the Clean Water Act, the Endangered Species Act, and state and local wetlands protection regulations.

However, despite the progress that has been made, natural habitat continues to be altered, degraded or lost. Our environment is far from static, and many uncertainties remain concerning the future of various bird species. Although the pace of development has slowed in Massachusetts, natural habitat continues to be lost on a daily basis. According to Mass Audubon estimates, approximately 22 acres of natural land were lost per day (8,030 acres per year) to development in Massachusetts between 1999 and 2005. Nationwide, that figure was approximately 6,000 acres per day (2.2 million per year) between 1982 and 2001 based on U.S. Forest Service data.

Our forest tracts are getting smaller and more fragmented by roads and other development. Birds that normally nest in forest interiors are losing habitat, as many of the wooded lots are becoming too small to provide sufficient food and nesting locations. In areas where forest interior birds do nest, they are increasingly subjected to nest predation from forest edge predators such as

Raccoons, and to brood parasitism by Brown-headed Cowbirds. Most birds that breed in forest interiors in our area overwinter in Central and South America, where they encounter even greater losses of habitat.

Natural habitats that remain are impacted by wastes and pollutants. Pesticides, toxic metals, petroleum, plastics, artificial light, greenhouse gases, and other contaminants are released into the environment as a result of human activities. Pesticides are found throughout our environment, including areas far from where they were used—such as the Arctic, the Antarctic, the air surrounding Mount Everest, and the deep sea. About 40 pesticides in use today are lethal to birds when applied as directed, including several chemicals that may be legally used in the United States. According to the U.S. Fish and Wildlife Service, an estimated 67 million birds are accidentally killed each year in the United States from acute exposure to pesticides used in agricultural areas. This number includes only those birds killed immediately; the total number is unknown. An unknown number of birds are also affected from chemicals used on lawns, which may contain up to 10 times more pesticides per acre than farmlands.[1]

Birds also die from ingestion of lead shot and lead fishing tackle left behind as litter. A single shotgun shell fired for the hunting of birds releases approximately 225 to 430 small lead pellets. The lead pellets are swallowed by birds, either incidentally while feeding off the ground or in the bottom substrate of lakes and ponds, or purposefully in order to aid in digestion.[2] Prior to 1991, millions of waterfowl died each year from lead poisoning after swallowing lead shot. Raptors, including Bald Eagles, were also poisoned after

---

[1] The notorious pesticide DDT, which was banned in the United States 40 years ago, is still used in about 18 countries to kill mosquitoes in areas where malaria is a problem (e.g., Venezuela, China, India, and parts of Africa). The Stockholm Convention, a global treaty to restrict and ultimately phase out persistent organic pollutants, currently permits the use of DDT for the control of mosquitoes and other disease vectors, as DDT is still one of the most effective, affordable means for saving human lives.

[2] Lacking teeth, many birds swallow grit (sand, pebbles, gravel) to grind food in their gizzard.

consuming waterfowl that had either been wounded with lead shot or had ingested it. In 1991, the U.S. Fish and Wildlife Service enacted a federal ban on the use or possession of lead shot while hunting waterfowl. Although some birds are still poisoned from consuming residual lead shot in water bodies, millions of waterfowl are now spared from lead poisoning.

However, lead shot continues to be used for the hunting of upland game birds and mammals. Upland game birds, especially Mourning Doves, are known to ingest lead shot while feeding. According to Schulz et al. (2006), as many as 15 million Mourning Doves may die each year from lead poisoning from ingestion of lead shot. Raptors, which benefited from the 1991 ban on lead shot for waterfowl hunting, may still be poisoned when they consume Mourning Doves or other upland birds or mammals containing lead shot.[3]

Lead fishing tackle, including sinkers and jigs (weighted hooks), left behind in water bodies may also poison birds. Although the amount of lead fishing tackle that ends up littering a water body is considerably less than the amount of lead shot formerly expelled into such areas, certain waterfowl, such as loons, swans, and ducks, may be adversely affected. Impacts may be substantial in water bodies that receive high recreational use. Ingestion of lead fishing tackle is currently the number one cause of death for adult Common Loons in New England. This situation is likely to change soon, as various states in the Northeast have recently adopted bans on the use and/or sale of lead fishing tackle (of sizes likely to be ingested by waterfowl). Bans went into effect in New Hampshire in 2000, in Maine in 2002, in New York in 2004, in Vermont in 2006 and 2007, and in Massachusetts in 2012.

Light pollution is a rapidly increasing and pervasive type of environmental pollution that affects wildlife, plants, and people. Artificial lights confuse and disorient birds that migrate at night.

---

[3] This is more of a concern in other parts of the country. Mourning Doves tend to feed in the same areas where they are hunted, resulting in their ingestion of substantial amounts of lead. Hunting is not allowed in Den Rock Park, and the hunting of Mourning Doves is prohibited in Massachusetts.

Birds navigate at night using methods that involve light—they observe light from the stars and other celestial objects to orient themselves, they also navigate using the earth's magnetic field through use of a light-dependent magnetic compass.

When artificial lights are present, birds tend to gravitate towards them. Like insects flying around a street light, migrating songbirds are known to fly in circles around lit up towers or buildings. Many birds collide with illuminated structures or they waste energy needed for migration on unnecessary flight.

Globally, hundreds of millions of nocturnally-migrating birds are adversely affected by artificial night lighting each year. In addition, artificial night lighting may affect the timing and duration of different bird behaviors. For example, American Robins normally begin singing at the start of dawn. However, in areas brightly illuminated at night they have been known to begin singing in the middle of the night. The long-term effects of such changes in behavior are largely unknown.

As of yet there are no Massachusetts state laws concerning outdoor-lighting.[4] A number of cities in the United States, including Boston, have voluntary Lights Out programs, whereby participating buildings turn off interior and exterior lights at night during spring and fall bird migration periods. (In Boston, lights are turned off between 11pm and 5am from March 1–June 1 and from August 15–October 31.) In addition to benefiting migrating birds, these measures help save money, reduce energy use, and decrease emissions of greenhouse gases.

Greenhouse gases, such as carbon dioxide, methane, and nitrous oxide, trap heat in the earth's atmosphere. Ice core data indicate that atmospheric concentrations of these gases have increased substantially over the past 250 years, with the most dramatic increases occurring during the past 50 years. Carbon dioxide, considered the most important greenhouse gas, has increased in the atmosphere primarily due to the burning of fossil fuels and

---

[4] Outdoor-lighting bills have been proposed in Massachusetts during every legislative session since 1992, but none have been passed as of this writing.

to a lesser extent from change in land use (i.e., clearing of land for agriculture, industry or other use). Concentrations of methane and nitrous oxide have increased mostly as a result of agriculture.

Evidence for global climate change caused by these surging greenhouse gas emissions is becoming ever more apparent. Global air and ocean temperatures have been increasing, the extent of Arctic sea ice has been decreasing, glaciers have been melting and losing volume, and global sea level has been rising. Other effects of climate change have been documented, including increases in ocean acidity, changes in wind patterns, and changes in precipitation and other weather patterns. In the northeastern United States, average air temperatures increased by almost 0.5 °F per decade since 1970, with average winter temperatures rising by more than 4 °F between 1970 and 2000. At the Arnold Arboretum in Jamaica Plain, plants are now flowering on average 8 days earlier than they did 100 years ago, coincident with a 2.7 °F increase in the average annual air temperature in Boston.

Additional warming is now considered inevitable over the next few decades as a result of the emissions that have already occurred. However, the severity of climate change in the long term will depend on the extent to which global emissions can be curtailed in the near future. If current warming trends continue, they will likely have profound impacts on habitats and food availability, and consequently on species' ranges, migrations, and survival.

Rapid development, advances in technology, and a trend towards globalization are accelerating the level of travel and trade between nations, making it increasingly more difficult to prevent the inadvertent introduction of foreign species, including viruses, bacteria, fungi, plants, and animals, which may potentially wreck havoc on native species and ecosystems.

Most species that are introduced to new ecosystems don't survive. Of the ones that do, most don't cause problems. However, a small percentage of introduced species may have damaging effects in their new environment. Non-native species that have harmful environmental or economic effects or adversely impact human health are considered invasive.

Species that become invasive are typically ones that grow and/or reproduce rapidly, are generalists with regards to habitat and food requirements, and have traits that allow them to be good competitors for resources. In their native ecosystems, the populations of such species are kept in check by biological and/or physical factors such as predators, diseases, climate conditions, competition with other similarly adapted species, and special adaptations of their prey or host species (e.g., evolved resistances or defenses). However, when a species is introduced to a new environment, many of the factors normally curtailing its growth may be absent, potentially enabling the organism to grow and spread uncontrollably.

Invasive species are considered the second greatest threat to birds, after the loss and degradation of habitat. Invasive species impact birds in a number of ways. Invasive plants displace native vegetation that birds rely on for food, nesting and shelter. They also support far fewer insects than do native plants, resulting in less food for birds to eat. Introduced pest species such as the Asian Long-horned Beetle, the Emerald Ash Borer, and the Hemlock Woolly Adelgid destroy forested habitat used by birds. Invasive European Starlings and House Sparrows outcompete native birds for nesting cavities. Exotic diseases such as West Nile virus kill birds of certain species. In addition, non-native predators kill large numbers of birds. House cats that roam outdoors are considered invasive species and are believed to kill hundreds of millions of songbirds each year in the United States.

The bird species that tend to be most affected by invasive organisms are ones that live on islands and species that are already rare for other reasons. However, invasive species may threaten any species. In a relatively short period of time, invasive disease-causing organisms can potentially exterminate species that are now common.[5]

---

[5] The Little Brown Bat was until recently the most common bat species in the Northeast. It is now in danger of extinction in our region due to a lethal fungal disease that apparently originated from Europe. White-nose syndrome first appeared in the United States in 2006 in a tourist cave in New York. Almost all of the bats in areas stricken by the disease have died (> 90 percent), and the disease continues to spread rapidly.

Increasing globalization is likely to result in more introductions of foreign species and more species becoming invasive. A greater mixing of the world's species will undoubtedly contribute to an accelerated rate of extinctions and a large loss of biodiversity. Climate change may exacerbate the problem of invasive species by enabling exotic species to colonize areas previously inhospitable to them and by making it possible for invasive pests (such as mosquito-borne pathogens) to remain active for a greater portion of the year (i.e., due to shorter milder winters).

In our ever-shrinking world, human/bird conflicts result in substantial impacts to certain populations of birds. Birds create problems for people when they become strike hazards to aircrafts, when they consume crops or cause other damage to agriculture, when they take fish from aquaculture facilities, and when they nest or roost in large numbers near human development. Millions of birds are killed each year in the United States to ensure public safety, to protect our food supplies, and to eliminate public nuisances. Millions more die accidentally as a result of collisions with glass buildings and windows, towers, vehicles, wires and lines. Birds are also killed in large numbers from entanglement in commercial fishing gear. Many of these impacts will be magnified in the future as the human population grows larger and per capita resource consumption continues to rise.

Technology is advancing at an ever-increasing rate, and new breakthroughs are likely to alter our lifestyles and perhaps our country's landscape and infrastructure. There is much uncertainty as to what our future world will look like and how it will accommodate birds and other wildlife. As human impacts to the earth grow larger, novel approaches and practices will be required by future generations to ensure sustainability—for ourselves and other species.

✷✷✷

The way we manage the landscape has a considerable effect on bird abundance and distribution. Where we create large fields, pastures, and meadows, grassland birds such as Bobolinks and Eastern Meadowlarks will benefit. In areas where extensive tracts of forest are preserved, interior forest species (e.g., warblers and thrushes) will have an opportunity to thrive. Where we create suburban neighborhoods, American Robins, American Crows, House Sparrows, and Northern Cardinals will dominate. Birds will move to areas where there is habitat and food for them, and when such areas are hard to come by, species will suffer declines. Given that humans largely control the natural landscape, birds are highly dependent on us for their survival.

Perhaps the only other species besides man that has the ability to create substantial habitat for birds is the beaver. Many if not most of the bird species that are found at Den Rock Park are present because of the habitat created by the beaver. However, the beaver pond is a temporary phenomenon. Once the beaver depletes its available supply of food, or conditions otherwise become unfavorable, it will move to a new location. By that time many of the dead trees that provided nesting and perching habitat in the pond will have fallen to the ground. The unmaintained beaver dam will erode and water will flow more freely out of the pond. The pond will gradually become transformed into marsh, and over time much of it will once again become forested. With the loss of habitat, the herons, ducks, swallows, and other Den Rock birds will take up seasonal residence elsewhere.

One day, after the trees have grown back, the beaver will return to reflood the area and the birds and other wildlife will reappear, in a cycle that hopefully will continue long into the future.

The Birds

The following 30 species of birds may be seen or heard in the park. A complete list of species is provided in Appendix B.

Canada Goose
Branta canadensis

Family: Anatidae (Geese, Swans, and Ducks)

Meaning of Scientific Name:
Branta – from the English *brant* for "burn," apparently referring to the color of the bird's plumage.
canadensis – Canadian

A Canada Goose in the Beaver Pond. May 4, 2010.

Diet: Submergent vegetation, grasses, winter wheat, clovers, and waste grain, especially corn.

Nest: On the ground near water. May nest on a stump, mound or muskrat lodge. The nest consists of a depression, approximately 16 to 25 inches in diameter, which is typically lined with sticks, reeds, grasses, and down. In Massachusetts, eggs are laid from April to June. One brood is raised per year. Nests may sometimes be parasitized by other Canada Geese (a behavior known as intraspecific brood parasitism).

History: Historically, Canada Geese were present in our area only during migration. They were long-distance migrants who bred in subarctic Canada. It is uncertain whether any Canada Geese bred in the eastern United States.

During the late 1800s, hunters began using live Canada Goose decoys to lure in this migratory game bird. They clipped the wings of the decoy birds so they were unable to fly away. The decoys were highly effective at attracting migrating geese, making it easy for hunters to shoot large numbers of birds.

In 1935, the federal government enacted a ban on live decoys because of plunging populations of waterfowl. Following this ban, many decoy geese were released into the wild. Having been raised in captivity for generations, the decoy geese never learned how to migrate, and became permanent residents. Lawns, golf courses, and other mowed grassy areas (especially ones with ponds) have provided ideal habitat for the feral geese—similar to the grassy tundra meadows of their ancestral breeding grounds. With abundant habitat and food, and minimal predation, numbers of feral geese have skyrocketed.

Although wild migrating populations of Canada Goose still pass through the state, the wild and feral populations tend to remain separate, as Canada Geese have a strong fidelity to their breeding grounds and normally return to their place of birth to breed.

Other Notes: Seven subspecies of Canada Goose have been identified: *Branta canadensis canadensis*, *B. c. interior*, *B. c. maxima*, *B. c. moffitti*, *B. c. parvipes*, *B. c. occidentalis*, and *B. c. fulva*. The feral/resident population of Canada Goose consists of a mixture of subspecies, including *B. c. canadensis*, *B. c. interior*, *B. c. maxima*, and *B. c. moffitti*, reflecting the different origins of the geese that were imported into this region for use as decoys.

Two migratory Canada Goose populations regularly occur in Massachusetts: the Atlantic Population (AP), consisting of *B. c. interior*, and the North Atlantic Population (NAP), consisting of *B. c. canadensis*.

AP geese breed in northern Quebec, primarily along the northeastern shore of Hudson Bay, and along the coast of Ungava Bay. Those that breed along the southern Ungava Bay coast migrate through eastern New York and western New England, including western Massachusetts. During fall migration they may be seen in western Massachusetts during October. Their wintering grounds are located mainly within the lower Hudson River drainage; a small number overwinter in western Massachusetts.

NAP geese nest mostly in Labrador and Newfoundland. They are a maritime population that usually remains within 10 miles of the coast. Fall migration occurs relatively late for these geese—generally they do not leave their nesting grounds until November or December.

NAP geese historically wintered along the Atlantic coast as far south as North Carolina. However, in recent years they have been wintering further north, with most now overwintering on Long Island and along the southern New England coastline, including Cape Cod and Buzzards Bay.

In addition to the AP and NAP geese, Canada Geese that nest in Greenland have been recently spotted in Massachusetts, perhaps indicating the start of a new migration pattern. During the winter of 2011/2012, Canada Geese with neck bands from Greenland were observed in Amherst (on the University of Massachusetts campus) and in South Egremont, Sheffield, and Concord.

Canada Geese may be legally hunted in Massachusetts by licensed hunters. Since 1995, Massachusetts has had special early (September) and late (January/February) hunting seasons for Canada Geese in addition to the regular fall hunting season. The early and late hunting seasons were added with the intention of targeting the feral/resident population of geese, which is often considered a nuisance. Since it is now known that many NAP geese winter along the southern Massachusetts coastline, that area is currently off-limits to hunters during the late Canada Goose season.

Feral/resident Canada Geese are commonly observed in Den Rock's Beaver Pond during spring, summer, and fall. During winter, they may be seen in the Shawsheen River. Parent geese with goslings have been observed in the Beaver Pond during May and June. When migrating, Canada Geese fly during the day and at night.

WOOD DUCK
Aix sponsa

Family: Anatidae (Geese, Swans, and Ducks)

Meaning of Scientific Name:
Aix – Greek for waterfowl
sponsa – Latin for betrothed. This likely refers to the male's plumage, which makes him appear as though he is dressed for a lavish wedding ceremony.

Diet: Mostly aquatic plants such as duckweed; also insects and other invertebrates, seeds, acorns, hickory nuts, berries, and grains.

Wood Duck male (top) and female.

Nest: Nests in tree cavities 3½ to 60 feet above ground or water, usually in a live tree. May use old woodpecker holes such as those of flickers, other natural cavities or nest boxes. Requires an entrance hole at least 3½ inches in diameter, while the inside cavity is at least 9 to 11 inches wide and 1 foot deep and it is lined with feathers. In Massachusetts, Wood Ducks lay eggs from mid-to-late March to late July and have one brood per year. Nests may be parasitized by other Wood Ducks.

History: Wood Ducks were formerly the most abundant duck in New England. They were intensely hunted for sale of their feathers, meat, and eggs. In addition, the clearing of land and draining of wetlands for agriculture eliminated much of their nesting habitat. By the early 1900s, the species was rendered nearly extinct.

In the 1930s, Wood Duck populations began to rebound as a result of a federal ban on the hunting of these ducks (enacted between 1918 and 1941) and an increase in nesting habitat. The return of the beaver and the decline of farming increased the availability of large cavity-containing trees needed for nesting. In addition, artificial nest boxes developed at that time were readily used by Wood Ducks. The federal Migratory Bird Treaty Act of 1918, which prohibited the market hunting of migratory birds, protected the Wood Duck from commercial exploitation once the hunting ban ended in 1941. The treaty also required that the hunting of game birds be regulated, with restricted hunting seasons to prevent adverse effects to populations. A large statewide nest box program during the early 1950s contributed to the Wood Duck's recovery.

Other Notes: "Egg dumping" (intraspecific brood parasitism) is a common behavior in Wood Ducks whereby a Wood Duck lays its eggs in the nest of another Wood Duck female. The host bird then incubates the eggs and raises the young along with her own. Approximately 30 percent of Wood Duck nests may be parasitized in this manner. A Wood Duck female that parasitizes another bird's nest may later establish a nest of her own. Sometimes Wood Ducks lay their eggs in the nests of Hooded Mergansers and vice versa.

Wood Ducks are frequently seen in Den Rock's Beaver Pond during early spring, typically from mid-March to early April, and also during August through October. In July 2012, a Wood Duck female with three ducklings was observed in the Beaver Pond.

Most Wood Ducks in Massachusetts are migratory and overwinter in the Carolinas and other areas in the southern United States. Wintering Wood Ducks may also be found along the coast as far north as Cape Cod. Migration occurs mainly at night. Wood Ducks usually arrive in Massachusetts in early to mid-March. During September and early October, prior to migration, Wood Ducks gather each night at roosts in wooded wetlands. Most Wood Ducks depart south during October or November.

The Massachusetts Division of Fisheries and Wildlife currently maintains over 1,600 Wood Duck nest boxes in the state. Wood Ducks may be legally hunted in Massachusetts by licensed hunters during the designated hunting season for ducks.

Mallard
Anas platyrhynchos

Family: Anatidae (Geese, Swans, and Ducks)

Meaning of Scientific Name:
Anas – Latin for duck
platyrhynchos (derived from Greek) – *platy* meaning flat or broad and *rhynchos* meaning bill

Male and female Mallards in the Beaver Pond. March 12, 2011.

Diet: Mostly aquatic vegetation; seeds of sedges, grasses, and smartweed; also grain, insects, acorns.

Nest: Built of grasses, leaves, and reeds. It has an inside diameter of 8 inches and is typically located on the ground near water. In Massachusetts, eggs are laid between early April and late July. Mallards have one brood per year. Mallard nests are occasionally parasitized by other ducks.

History: During the early 1900s, Mallards were uncommon in Massachusetts and did not breed here. They occurred in the central portion of the country, with their breeding grounds located mostly west of Hudson Bay. Mallards are reported to have increased in Massachusetts beginning in the 1920s. They were imported, propagated, and released in this area to supplement the natural populations of ducks available for hunting. In 1935, a number of Mallards were also released into the wild when the United States government instituted a federal ban on the use of live decoys for hunting.

In addition to the introduction of these feral birds, since the late 1800s or early 1900s, Mallard have been expanding their range east, with more birds arriving here naturally on their own. Currently, Mallards are the most abundant waterfowl in Massachusetts and the United States.

Mallards readily interbreed and produce fertile hybrids with the American Black Duck. Given the abundance of the Mallard and the decline of the American Black Duck in the Northeast, there is concern that this hybridization may threaten the existence of the American Black Duck. A similar situation is occurring in Florida, where feral Mallards are interbreeding with Florida Mottled Ducks and threatening their future existence.

Other Notes: Mallards may be spotted in the Shawsheen River year-round, and in the Beaver Pond from spring to fall, as long as there is open water in the pond. Females with ducklings have been observed in the Beaver Pond during late May and early June.

Mallards may be legally hunted in Massachusetts by licensed hunters during the designated hunting season for ducks.

GREAT BLUE HERON
Ardea herodias

Family: Ardeidae (Bitterns and Herons)

Meaning of Scientific Name:
Ardea – Latin for heron
herodias – Greek for heron

Diet: Small fish, frogs, birds, and aquatic insects.

Nest: In Massachusetts, usually nests in colonies in beaver ponds. Builds a platform of large sticks, small branches and twigs, usually at the top of tall trees. The nest generally has an outside diameter of

2 to 3½ feet. The inside is lined with leaves and fine twigs. Eggs are laid between early April and late May in Massachusetts, and one brood is raised per year.

An adult Great Blue Heron eating a fish in the Beaver Pond. April 1, 2010. Adult Great Blue Herons have a white patch at the top of the head and both mandibles of the bill are orangish.

History: Prior to the federal Migratory Bird Treaty Act of 1918, the Great Blue Heron was widely hunted for its feathers, which were used in the millinery (hat) trade.

During the late 1800s and early 1900s, the Great Blue Heron was reported to be a common migrant in Massachusetts, although it was only rarely observed during summer and winter. The first documented nesting of Great Blue Heron in Massachusetts occurred in 1925, in Harvard Forest in Petersham. However, a 1912 birding guide by Albert Morse noted that the Great Blue Heron formerly bred in eastern Massachusetts. According to Griscom and Snyder (1955), it was a "rare and extirpated" summer resident in the state.

Recently, numbers of Great Blue Herons have increased dramatically in Massachusetts, probably due to an expansion in the beaver population.[1]

Other Notes: Great Blue Herons are commonly seen in Den Rock's Beaver Pond, catching fish and other prey. They are typically observed in the pond or in trees along the water's edge from

---

[1] The beaver population experienced rapid growth after 1996, when Massachusetts banned the use, setting, placement, maintenance, manufacturing, and possession of body-gripping traps for capturing fur-bearing mammals. These traps, considered inhumane, are now only used in emergency situations and require a permit.

early spring through fall. According to locals, Great Blue Herons formerly nested in the Beaver Pond; however, the tree used for nesting has since fallen down.

Both migratory and overwintering Great Blue Herons occur in New England. Migratory herons arrive in New England in the latter part of March and fly south from mid-July to late September, traveling during day and night. They spend the winter along the Atlantic coast, from Massachusetts to the West Indies. Some herons overwinter in New England in coastal areas with snow-free ground and open water, or in areas where freshwater remains open.

During the winter of 2009/2010, an immature Great Blue Heron was observed ice-fishing in the Beaver Pond at Den Rock Park on a regular basis. The heron routinely fished at the western edge of the pond by Stirling Street, where water flows into the pond via a culvert. In this area there were openings in the ice where the bird was able to hunt. The heron was observed fishing at the same location from January until the spring ice melt in March.

An immature Great Blue Heron ice-fishing in the Beaver Pond. February 22, 2010. On this particular date the bird was observed standing over a hole that had frozen over. Immature Great Blue Herons have an all-dark head (no white patch) and a dark upper mandible.

Green Heron
Butorides virescens

Family: Ardeidae (Bitterns and Herons)

Meaning of Scientific Name:
Butorides – from the Latin word *butio*, for bittern, and the Greek *eidos*, meaning resembling
virescens – becoming green (Latin)

A Green Heron in the Beaver Pond. June 1, 2011.

Diet: Primarily small fish; also insects, other invertebrates, reptiles, and amphibians. The Green Heron has been known to use bait (e.g., insects, twigs) to attract fish.

Nest: In a tree or shrub typically 10 to 30 feet above ground, often near water. The nest has an outside diameter of 10 to 12 inches. It is usually concealed and is constructed of interwoven twigs and sticks. Generally nests singly; sometimes nests in a loose colony. In Massachusetts, lays eggs between early May and mid-June and has one brood per year.

History: During the late 1800s and early 1900s the Green Heron was reported to be a common summer resident in Massachusetts. It experienced a gradual decline after 1910, believed to be due to the widespread filling of wetlands. The Green Heron was also hunted for its meat. During the 1950s it was considered uncommon in the

Andover area. Currently, the Green Heron has a wide distribution in Massachusetts during the summer and is fairly common in our area.

Other Notes: This heron is occasionally observed in Den Rock's Beaver Pond during spring and summer, feeding on small fish and other prey. The Green Heron is migratory and usually flies at night, arriving in Massachusetts in late April and departing in late September through mid-October. It winters in the southern United States and south to northern South America.

According to Breeding Bird Survey data, numbers of Green Herons observed in Massachusetts have declined over the past few decades. The Green Heron is currently considered a species of conservation concern in Massachusetts (MassWildlife, 2006).

BLACK-CROWNED NIGHT-HERON
Nycticorax nycticorax

Family: Ardeidae (Bitterns and Herons)

Meaning of Scientific Name:

Nycticorax – From the prefix *nycti-* meaning night and the Greek word *corax* for raven or crow (in reference to its nocturnal habits and raven-like call).

The elusive Black-crowned Night-heron in Den Rock's Beaver Pond. August 17, 2011.

Diet: Fish, crustaceans, mollusks, worms, leeches, insects, reptiles and amphibians, and occasionally young birds and mammals. Feeds at dawn and dusk, and during the early part of the night. Forages in saltwater and freshwater environments.

Nest: Nests in colonies, mainly along the coast and often with other species. The nests are built in shrubs or trees approximately 7 to 15 above ground in wooded swamps and shrub swamps, or they may be located in cattails or stands of Common Reed. They are made of sticks, twigs, and reeds and have an outside diameter of approximately 2 feet. In Massachusetts, eggs are laid from early to mid-April to late June and one brood is raised per year.

History: In the past, the Black-crowned Night-heron was the most common heron in our area. During the 1900s it suffered declines as a result of habitat loss, human persecution, and DDT.

Black-crowned Night-heron rookeries have long been considered a nuisance due to their noise and droppings. The droppings or guano are known to produce odors, damage vegetation, corrode metal, and potentially provide a substrate for a disease-causing fungus.

The Black-crowned Night-heron is regarded as especially troublesome when it nests near hydroelectric dams and other developments. It is considered a pest at aquaculture facilities where it is known to take fish. It is also considered a problem when it predates the nests of rare species of terns, including the federally-endangered Roseate Tern. The Black-crowned Night-heron is protected under the Migratory Bird Treaty Act and cannot be killed without a federal permit. A permit may be obtained only if damage caused by the birds cannot be controlled using non-lethal means.

Locally the Black-crowned Night-heron once nested along the Merrimack River in Haverhill and Lowell. In Oscar Root's *The Birds of the Andover Region*, the Black-crowned Night-heron is described as formerly nesting in colonies at Ward Hill Neck in Haverhill. Today, Ward Hill Neck is the site of a landfill and energy-from-waste incinerator.

According to the City of Lowell's *Comprehensive Master Plan Existing Conditions Report* (2002), a Black-crowned Night-heron rookery was located until recently at the foot of the Pawtucket Falls in the Merrimack River, by Beaver Brook. However, the birds abandoned the site after a sewer interceptor was constructed and nesting trees were vandalized. According to Massachusetts Breeding Bird Atlas data, known breeding areas for Black-crowned Night-herons in Massachusetts are currently located exclusively along the coast. Since the 1920s, the numbers of breeding pairs in coastal areas of the state have declined substantially.

Although the Black-crowned Night-heron is not currently protected under the Massachusetts Endangered Species Act, it is listed as a species of conservation concern in the Massachusetts State Wildlife Action Plan (MassWildlife, 2006). Mass Audubon's 2011 *State of the Birds* report identifies it as a species in urgent need of conservation action.

Other Notes: The Black-crowned Night-heron is very widely distributed and breeds on all continents except Antarctica and Australia. It is migratory and overwinters in southern New England and further south. This heron usually arrives in Massachusetts in mid-March. At the end of the nesting season, adult and juvenile birds disperse, typically beginning in mid- to late July. It is usually around this time (July and August) that Black-crowned Night-herons are spotted at Den Rock Park. They forage in the Beaver Pond, and may be seen during the evening or morning hours. Black-crowned Night-herons migrate south during October and November, flying mainly at night.

Red-tailed Hawk
Buteo jamaicensis

Family: Accipitridae (Kites, Eagles, and Hawks)

Meaning of Scientific Name:
Buteo – a kind of falcon or hawk (Latin)
jamaicensis – of Jamaica

Red-tailed Hawks in a dead tree along the edge of the Beaver Pond. August 4, 2007.

Diet: Small mammals, especially rodents; also birds, reptiles, amphibians, insects, crayfish, and carrion.

Nest: In a tree 35 to 90 feet above ground, made of sticks and twigs and lined with grapevine and cedar bark, moss, and evergreen sprigs. The nest has an outside diameter of 28 to 38 inches (inside diameter of 14 to 15 inches). In Massachusetts, eggs are laid between late March and late April with one brood per year.

History: Historically, the Red-tailed Hawk and other birds of prey were considered "varmints" and were trapped and shot in large numbers. They were despised by farmers who considered them threats to their chickens and other livestock. The Red-tailed Hawk was sometimes referred to as a "Hen Hawk" for its occasional habit of taking hens. During the 1700s and 1800s bounties were established in various municipalities in order to eradicate "undesirable" species such as "Hen Hawks." Under the bounty system, a hunter was paid for each dead hawk that he brought back. Normally just the head of the animal was brought in for collection of the bounty.

Red-tailed Hawks and several other raptor species undergo spectacular migrations during the fall. Many follow mountain ridges during their journey south, where they are able to take advantage of thermals and updrafts and thereby expend very little energy during their flights. During the fall, several thousand hawks pass by mountains in the Northeast including Mount Agamenticus in Maine, Mount Wachusett in Massachusetts and Hawk Mountain in Pennsylvania. In the past, hunters would come to the tops of such mountains during migrations and shoot hawks for sport, killing them by the hundreds, and at some locations by the thousands.

Needless to say, by the early 1900s Red-tailed Hawks were rare in our area. The Migratory Bird Treaty Act of 1918 provided no protection to Red-tailed Hawks or other birds of prey, as they were still considered "varmints" at that time. It wasn't until 1972 that birds of prey received federal protection.

Other Notes: Over the past several decades, Red-tailed Hawks have been increasing in Massachusetts as a result of their federal protection from hunting, their adaptability to living near people, and an abundance of habitat suitable to them (i.e., open areas for hunting with scattered trees and small woodlots for perching and nesting). Currently, Red-tailed Hawks are common in our area. Fall migration occurs between September and December. During this time summits and ridge tops are now covered with hawk-watchers rather than hunters. The spring hawk migration, which takes place between March and May, is less of a spectacle in Massachusetts, as fewer hawks are seen at any given time or place. Some Red-tailed Hawks remain in Massachusetts throughout the year, and others that breed farther north may overwinter here. The winter range for Red-tailed Hawks extends as far south as northern South America and as far north as southern Canada. The Red-tailed Hawk's breeding range includes most of North America and parts of Central America.

Red-tailed Hawks are seen year-round at the Beaver Pond, either gliding overhead or perched in trees along the edge of the pond.

MOURNING DOVE
Zenaida macroura

Family: Columbidae (Pigeons and Doves)

Meaning of Scientific Name:
Zenaida – Name given by French zoologist Charles L. Bonaparte in 1838 in honor of his wife, Princess Zénaide (they were niece and nephew to Napoleon Bonaparte). *macroura* (Greek) – from *macros* meaning long and *oura* meaning tail.

Mourning Doves on a perch in the Beaver Pond. March 21, 2010.

Diet: Almost entirely seeds, including weed, grass, and grain seeds. Both parents produce a nutritious substance known as crop milk or pigeon milk, which is regurgitated and fed to nestlings. (Crop milk is said to have the consistency and smell of cottage cheese.)

By July and August, near the end of their breeding period, Mourning Doves may appear especially abundant in the Beaver Pond. A high reproductive rate is normal and necessary for this species to compensate for its high mortality rate. Photo taken July 11, 2010.

Nest: A loosely assembled platform of sticks, twigs, grasses and weeds in a tree (usually evergreen), generally 10 to 25 feet above ground. May also nest in tangles of shrubs or vines. Nest has little if any lining and has an outside diameter of 8 to 12 inches. May use abandoned nests of other species as a foundation for its nest. Eggs are generally laid between mid-April and late July in Massachusetts. Mourning Doves have two or more broods per year. The nests are rarely parasitized by cowbirds, and any cowbird egg accepted into a Mourning Dove nest would be unlikely to survive.[2]

History: Mourning doves were extensively hunted during the late 1800s. By around 1900 they were considered "very rare" summer residents in the Andover area. The Passenger Pigeon, a close relative of the Mourning Dove, was also heavily hunted during the same period and was extirpated from the state by 1894, eventually becoming extinct. In 1908, Massachusetts banned the hunting of Mourning Doves in order to prevent this species from meeting the same fate as the Passenger Pigeon. Since 1920, numbers of Mourning Doves in Massachusetts have rebounded.

Other Notes: The hunting of Mourning Doves is still prohibited in Massachusetts, as well as in seven other states.[3] However, Mourning Doves are now hunted in the 40 other states in which they occur. Mourning Doves are hunted more than any other game bird in North America (approximately 20 million birds are bagged per year in the United States), and their annual harvest exceeds that of all the other migratory game birds combined.

Mourning Doves are among the most abundant birds in the United States. Their populations are highly dynamic, with 50 to 75 percent of a given population dying each year. Numbers of Mourning Doves increase dramatically during the breeding season, from spring to late summer.

At Den Rock Park, Mourning Doves are commonly observed in the Beaver Pond between March and October. They frequently perch on dead trees in the pond, and in the past have nested in the pines bordering the pond. Many Mourning Doves are permanent

---

[2] Mourning Doves are improper hosts because of the unusual manner in which the chick feeds (i.e., by actively inserting its bill into the adult's throat rather than waiting with an open mouth to be fed) and because the type of food provided (i.e., crop milk and seeds) would probably not sustain a cowbird.

[3] Connecticut, Maine, Michigan, New Hampshire, New Jersey, New York, and Vermont do not allow the hunting of Mourning Doves.

residents in Massachusetts although some do migrate. Migrating Mourning Doves fly during the day and overwinter in the southeastern United States, returning to Massachusetts during late February or early March. Fall migration begins in September, with most migrants gone by December.

BELTED KINGFISHER
Megaceryle alcyon

Family: Alcedinidae (Kingfishers)

Meaning of Scientific Name:
Megaceryle – from the Greek *mega* meaning large or great and *kerylos* meaning seabird
alcyon – named after Alkyon from Greek mythology—she was turned into a kingfisher.

A Belted Kingfisher on a branch in the Beaver Pond. April 19, 2010.

Diet: Fish, amphibians, reptiles, insects. Undigested remains are regurgitated in pellets.

Nest: Excavates a burrow in a sandy bank, usually near water. The entrance hole is 3 to 4 inches in diameter and is generally 1 to 3 feet below the top of a cutaway bank. The tunnel may be as long as 15 feet. In Massachusetts, eggs are laid between mid-May and the first week in June, with one brood raised per year.

History: Accounts from the early 1900s describe the Belted Kingfisher as being a common summer resident in our area. Based on Massachusetts Breeding Bird Atlas data, the kingfisher has become a more widespread breeder within the state during the past few decades.

Other Notes: Belted Kingfishers may be encountered in Den Rock's Beaver Pond during spring and summer. They are usually observed in the pond by the second week in April. Kingfishers may also be occasionally seen by the Shawsheen River. The kingfisher's rattle-like chattering call is often heard before the bird is spotted.

Kingfishers are present in Massachusetts throughout the year. During winter they tend to occur along the coast, although some birds may be found inland if open water is present. Some Belted Kingfishers migrate, and overwinter in the southern United States to as far south as northern South America.

Red-bellied Woodpecker
Melanerpes carolinus

Family: Picidae (Woodpeckers)

Meaning of Scientific Name:
Melanerpes – derived from the Greek words *melas*, meaning black, and *herpes*, meaning creeper.
carolinus – of [North or South] Carolina

Diet: Wood-boring and other insects on trunks and limbs of trees; also fruit, berries, seeds and acorns.

A Red-bellied Woodpecker in a tree along the edge of the Beaver Pond. February 14, 2010.

Nest: Excavates a hole in a dead tree or branch, stump, utility pole or wooden building. Also uses nest boxes. The nest cavity is usually less than 40 feet above ground, with an entry hole 1¾ to 2¼ inches in diameter and a depth of 12 inches. In the Northeast (New York), eggs are laid between late April and late June with one brood per year. Starlings are fierce competitors for nest sites and often steal the nest holes once they are completed.

History: Traditionally a bird of the southeastern United States, Red-bellied Woodpeckers only recently expanded their range north into New England. Prior to 1955 they were considered rare vagrants in Massachusetts. They nested for the first time in Connecticut in 1962, and in Massachusetts in 1977. Since then, their breeding population in Massachusetts has increased enormously. Red-bellied Woodpeckers have also been expanding their range westward. Possible explanations for the range expansion have included an increase in backyard bird feeders and increased suburbanization. The Red-bellied Woodpecker is a habitat generalist and adapts well to living in suburban areas.

Other Notes: This woodpecker may be observed year-round at Den Rock Park and is most commonly seen at the western edge of the Beaver Pond. Its rolling "Kwir" call is often heard. Red-bellied Woodpeckers are generally considered non-migratory.

DOWNY WOODPECKER
Picoides pubescens

Family: Picidae (Woodpeckers)

Meaning of Scientific Name:
Picoides – from the Latin word *picus*, for woodpecker
pubescens – downy (Latin)

Diet: A variety of insects, especially wood-boring. Also consumes fruit, seeds, and sap from sapsucker holes.

Nest: Excavates a nest cavity in a dead tree 5 to 40 feet above ground. The entrance is 1¼ inches in diameter and the hole extends downward

A Downy Woodpecker on a dead tree in the Beaver Pond. April 19, 2010.

8 to 10 inches. In Massachusetts, eggs are laid between mid-to-late May and mid-to-late June with one brood raised per year. In the fall each bird excavates a new hole for winter roosts. A bird house may occasionally be used for roosting but not for nesting.

History: The abundance and distribution of this woodpecker have remained fairly constant over time. It has been considered a common bird in our area since at least the late 1800s/early 1900s.

Other Notes: The Downy Woodpecker is the smallest North American woodpecker. It occurs throughout most of the United States and forested portions of Canada. The Downy Woodpecker may be seen or heard at Den Rock Park throughout the year. It is commonly found on trees in or along the edge of the Beaver Pond and in the oak forest. Downy Woodpeckers are not known to migrate.

HAIRY WOODPECKER
Picoides villosus

Family: Picidae (Woodpeckers)

Meaning of Scientific Name:
Picoides – from the Latin word *picus*, for woodpecker
villosus – covered with soft hairs (Latin)

Diet: A variety of insects, especially wood-boring beetles and larvae, ants, and caterpillars. It also eats fruits, nuts, and corn. Its winter diet includes acorns and hazelnuts.

Nest: Excavates a nest cavity in a live or dead tree, often an oak or aspen that has a diameter at breast height of at least 8 to 10 inches. The nest cavity is typically 10 to 40 feet above ground and the entrance hole is usually 2½ inches high and 2 inches wide. House Sparrows and European Starlings often steal the nest cavities. In Massachusetts, Hairy Woodpeckers lay eggs between mid-to-late April and late May. One or two broods are raised per year.

History: Like the Downy Woodpecker, the Hairy Woodpecker has been present in our area throughout the known past. However, it has generally been reported to be less abundant than the Downy Woodpecker. Within eastern North America, Hairy Woodpecker populations appear to be experiencing a slight but steady decline.

A Hairy Woodpecker in the Beaver Pond. June 17, 2010.

Other Notes: The Hairy Woodpecker is similar in appearance to the Downy Woodpecker, but it is larger and has a longer bill relative to the size of its head. It has a wider distribution than the Downy Woodpecker, and occurs throughout much of forested North America, with its range extending to southern Central America.

The Hairy Woodpecker is considered a forest-interior species, and increasing forest fragmentation is believed to be responsible for declines in populations. It requires larger, more mature trees and more expansive wooded areas for nesting than the closely related Downy Woodpecker. The Hairy Woodpecker has an estimated home range of at least 6 to 8 acres on which it may remain for life. At Den Rock Park, Hairy Woodpeckers may be seen and/or heard throughout the year in the oak forest. They are also occasionally observed on dead trees in the Beaver Pond. Hairy Woodpeckers are generally considered non-migratory.

Northern Flicker
Colaptes auratus

Family: Picidae (Woodpeckers)

Meaning of Scientific Name:
Colaptes – derived from the Greek word *kolapto*, meaning to peck with the bill.
auratus – meaning ornamented with gold (Latin)

Diet: Primarily ants. Also catches insects in the air and eats ground beetles, crickets, grasshoppers, fruit, berries, seeds, acorns, nuts, and grain.

Nest: Excavates a round hole approximately 2 to 4 inches in diameter in a large dead or dying tree usually 10 to 30 feet above ground. May use nest boxes. In Massachusetts, eggs are laid between mid-to-late April and mid-June with one brood raised per year. Nest cavities may be taken over by starlings and squirrels.

History: For over 100 years the Northern Flicker was considered a common summer resident in our area

Northern Flickers on a dead tree in the Beaver Pond. April 9, 2009.

and it is still considered common today. However, since 1966 its populations have been significantly declining in the United States based on Breeding Bird Survey data. The reasons for the decline are unknown, but may include competition with starlings for nest cavities, a decrease in the number of dead trees available for nesting (due to increased suburbanization and the lack of dead trees in such areas), and pesticide use on golf courses, farm fields, and lawns.

Other Notes: The Northern Flicker is considered an ecologically important species because it excavates a large number of the nest cavities that are eventually used by other species, and because it is a primary predator of ants. The flicker is a forest edge species, and has generally adapted well to living in areas impacted by people. Most flickers in our area are migratory and overwinter in the southern United States. Migration is believed to occur mainly at night. Spring migration occurs during April, and peak fall migration takes place in late September through October. Some flickers are permanent residents and generally spend the winter in coniferous forests or swamps along the coast. During spring and summer, Northern Flickers may be observed on dead trees in Den Rock Park's Beaver Pond where they have been known to nest.

EASTERN PHOEBE
Sayornis phoebe

Family: Tyrannidae (Tyrant Flycatchers)

Meaning of Scientific Name:
Sayornis – named after the American naturalist Thomas Say. *Ornis* is Greek for bird.
phoebe – named for the sound of the bird's call.

Diet: Flying insects.

Nest: Built on shelf-like projections of buildings, bridges or other man-made structures, or plastered to rocky ledges, upturned roots, or concrete or wooden walls. The nest has an outside diameter of 4½ inches (inside diameter of 2½ inches) and is built of grasses, weeds, mosses, and mud.

An Eastern Phoebe on a branch in the Beaver Pond. August 17, 2011.

It is often located close to open water where flying insects are plentiful. In Massachusetts, eggs are laid between late April and mid-August and two broods are raised per year. Nests are commonly parasitized by cowbirds.

History: During the late 1800s and early 1900s the phoebe was described as common or very common in our area. By 1952, the phoebe was considered uncommon. The decline in phoebe populations was believed to be due at least in part to the loss of farmland during this time. Phoebes were plentiful when the land was mostly cleared, and insects were available in abundance in fields. As the land became more forested, suitable habitat for phoebes decreased. DDT probably also played a role in the decline of the phoebe.

DDT, which became commercially available in the United States after World War II, was mainly used from the late 1940s through the 1960s. In Massachusetts, DDT was sprayed to control Gypsy Moth Caterpillars, to kill mosquitoes, and to thwart the spread of Dutch Elm Disease, in addition to its agricultural application. In *Silent Spring*, Rachel Carson described reported scarcities of phoebes and other flycatchers following DDT spraying. The decline of these birds was thought to be due to the lack of insects and/or the consumption of poisoned insects.

Today Eastern Phoebes are common and widespread breeders in Massachusetts. They have become well adapted to living and nesting in areas near people.

Other Notes: One of the first signs of spring at Den Rock Park is the arrival of the Eastern Phoebes. Most Eastern Phoebes overwinter in the southeastern United States, with the first spring migrants appearing in Massachusetts during early March. Although not frequently seen, they announce their presence with their loud gruff "feebee" calls (not to be confused with the sweet whistled "feebee" song of the Black-capped Chickadee). The calls are usually heard at Den Rock Park in the vicinity of the Stirling Street neighborhood from late March to early May. Phoebes may be occasionally spotted fly-catching from perches in the Beaver Pond. While perched they have a distinctive habit of bobbing their tail up and down.

Peak fall migration for phoebes takes place during late September or early October. Phoebes tend to be solitary birds and usually migrate individually rather than in flocks.

EASTERN KINGBIRD
Tyrannus tyrannus

Family: Tyrannidae (Tyrant Flycatchers)

Meaning of Scientific Name:
Tyrannus – tyrant or absolute ruler (Latin)

Diet: Primarily flying insects. Commonly feeds over open water or land. During winter eats mostly fruit.

Nest: Loosely constructed of weeds, moss, bark, or other soft materials and with an inside diameter of 3 inches. Usually located near the tip of a horizontal branch at a height of 10 to 20 feet above water, or occasionally on tops of stumps in water.

An Eastern Kingbird on a perch in the Beaver Pond. May 4, 2010.

In Massachusetts, kingbirds lay eggs between late May and early July and have one brood per year. Nests are commonly parasitized by cowbirds but the cowbird eggs are usually thrown out or damaged.

History: Like the Eastern Phoebe, the Eastern Kingbird was relatively common in the Andover area during the late 1800s and early 1900s and then experienced a decrease in abundance by the mid-1900s. Loss of habitat associated with the decline in farming and the widespread use of DDT likely contributed to its decrease. Like the phoebe, the kingbird has adapted to living in suburban areas and is currently common and widespread in our area.

Other Notes: The Eastern Kingbird is known for its aggressive territorial behavior, particularly towards large birds and birds of prey, including hawks, crows, and owls. It may be observed in Den Rock Park during spring and summer, flying after insects from perches in the Beaver Pond.

Eastern Kingbirds are migratory and spend the winter in northern South America. In their wintering grounds they are gregarious, nonterritorial fruit-eaters. Kingbirds generally arrive in Massachusetts during the first week in May. During late summer they congregate along the coast, with most birds departing the area by mid-September. Migration occurs during the day.

BLUE JAY
Cyanocitta cristata

Family: Corvidae (Jays, Magpies and Crows)

Meaning of Scientific Name:
Cyanocitta – from the Greek *kyanos*, meaning blue, and *kitta*, meaning jay.
cristata – crested (Latin)

Diet: Acorns and other nuts, seeds, fruit, insects, bird eggs and nestlings.

Blue Jay

Nest: The nest is generally well hidden in a crotch or outer branch of a tree (usually evergreen), typically 10 to 25 feet above ground. It has an outside diameter of 7 to 8 inches (inside diameter of 3½ to 4 inches) and is constructed of twigs, bark, leaves and man-made materials (e.g., string), with a lining of rootlets. In Massachusetts, eggs are laid between late April and mid-June and one brood is raised per year. Blue Jay nests are rarely parasitized by cowbirds, and any cowbird egg laid in a Blue Jay nest is almost always rejected.

History: Throughout known history Blue Jays have been common in our area. They are considered very intelligent birds and have adapted well to living in areas modified by people. In the past they were considered agricultural pests, given their fondness for corn and other crops, and were often shot by farmers. They are still thought of as pests today in some areas, although the crop damage they cause is considered minor compared to that of some other species. Crops impacted by Blue Jays include pecans and hazelnuts. Originally, Blue Jays were confined to the eastern portion of North America, east of the Great Plains. Since the mid-1900s, they have expanded their range westward. They have now been observed in all of the contiguous United States. Their range expansion is believed to be associated with westward development.

Other Notes: Blue Jays may be seen and heard throughout the year at Den Rock Park. The oak forest at Den Rock provides an important food source for this species, as acorns are a staple in the Blue Jay's diet. During fall, Blue Jays harvest acorns and other nuts from trees. The nuts that are not immediately eaten are carried off and then buried for later retrieval. A single Blue Jay may cache 3,000 or more acorns during one season. Given that some of the nuts will go unrecovered and eventually germinate, Blue Jays may serve as important dispersal agents for oaks and other nut-bearing trees.

A Blue Jay on a tree in the Beaver Pond. March 11, 2010.

The Blue Jays seen in our area include permanent residents and short-distance migrants. Migrating jays are generally observed passing through Massachusetts during late May, and from September through November. Migratory flights occur during the day. All Blue Jays are believed to overwinter in North America.

AMERICAN CROW
Corvus brachyrhynchos

Family: Corvidae (Jays, Magpies and Crows)

Meaning of Scientific Name:
Corvus – from the Latin word for raven or crow
brachyrhynchos – derived from the Greek *brachy* meaning short, and *rhynchos* meaning bill

American Crow

Diet: Cultivated grains (especially corn), seeds, fruits, nuts, insects and other invertebrates, carrion, bird eggs, nestlings, and other small vertebrates. Caches surplus food.

Nest: Builds a platform/basket nest of sticks and twigs usually 20 to 60 feet above ground on a tree. Typically nests in the tops of pines or oaks near clearings. The nest has an outside diameter of 24 inches (inside diameter of 7 inches) and is lined with shredded bark, grasses or other soft materials. Crow nests are rarely parasitized by cowbirds. In Massachusetts, eggs are laid between early May and mid-June and one brood is raised per year.

History: Since colonial times, crows have managed to thrive in areas populated by people. Being highly intelligent and opportunistic, crows adapted well to living in human-altered landscapes, where they have learned to find an abundance of food. In the past crows were considered major agricultural pests and were often shot. A number of towns in Massachusetts offered bounties for crows.

As agricultural areas spread throughout the United States, crows expanded their range and multiplied. In the Midwest and Great Plains, where crows were a scourge to farmers, crow roosting areas, containing thousands of birds, were dynamited. During the Great Depression, the United States government provided free ammunition to farmers to shoot crows. Other control methods for crows included trapping and poisoning.

The original Migratory Bird Treaty Act of 1918, which prohibited the hunting of native non-game birds, did not provide any protection to the American Crow. Although it is native and not a game species, it was considered a "varmint" and was hunted without restriction. It wasn't until 1972 that crows received federal protection. However, although the crow is now protected under the Migratory Bird Treaty Act, it may still be hunted even though it is not considered a game bird.

U.S. Fish and Wildlife Service regulations (50 CFR 20.133) allow states other than Hawaii[4] to establish their own hunting regulations for crows, given the following restrictions (1) crows are not hunted from aircraft (2) the hunting season does not exceed a total of 124 days per calendar year (3) hunting does not occur during the peak crow nesting period within a state; and (4) crows are killed only by firearms, bow and arrow, and falconry.

Currently crows may be legally hunted in Massachusetts by licensed hunters, with no bag limits. They may be hunted on three designated days of the week for most of the year, excluding their nesting season. Crows are not normally eaten or used for any purpose, but are typically shot because they are considered a nuisance or for target practice.

Under the *Depredation order for blackbirds, cowbirds, grackles, crows, and magpies* (50 CFR 21.43), crows may be killed without a federal permit (or hunting license) if they are causing damage or are about to cause damage to ornamental or shade trees, agricultural crops, livestock, or wildlife, or if they are considered a health hazard or other nuisance and cannot be controlled using non-lethal means. The federal depredation order regulations now stipulate reporting requirements and other conditions, and the killing of crows under this order may only be undertaken if also

---

[4] The Hawaiian Crow *(Corvus hawaiiensis)* is the only crow species in Hawaii and it is on the brink of extinction. Currently, it occurs only in captivity.

allowed under state regulations. Since January 2011, the U.S. Fish and Wildlife Service has required the use of non-toxic shot or non-toxic bullets when firearms are used to control pest birds under this order. However, lead ammunition may still be used when crows are hunted for sport.

Today crows are considered less of an agricultural pest than in previous times. Other species, including Brown-headed Cowbirds and Red-winged Blackbirds, are persecuted under the depredation order regulations on a much larger scale.

From 2009 through 2011, approximately 10,000 crows were killed per year by U.S. Department of Agriculture (USDA) Animal and Plant Health Inspection Services (APHIS) Wildlife Services personnel. Most of the animals were killed using firearms or through the use of bait laced with the slow-acting avian poison DRC-1339. Crows may be killed when they cause or are about to cause agricultural damage, when they roost in urban areas and their noise and droppings are considered a nuisance, and when they prey on federally-listed threatened or endangered species. In Massachusetts crows have been poisoned using DRC-1339 because they predate eggs and nestlings of the federally-threatened Piping Plover.

A lone crow on a perch overlooking the Beaver Pond. March 12, 2011.

Other Notes: Crows may be seen and heard in the vicinity of Den Rock's Beaver Pond throughout the year. Most American Crows in Massachusetts are permanent residents; however, northern populations are migratory, with migration occurring during the day. Migrating crows may be observed in Massachusetts during March and October. All American Crows overwinter in North America.

During spring and summer, crows occur in small family groups. In many crow populations, including ones observed in the Northeast, young crows may remain with their parents for four or more years, assisting with nest building and care of their younger siblings. During fall and winter, crows move about in large roaming flocks. During this time they assemble for the night in communal roosts, usually in dense stands of white pine. The roosting areas may contain thousands of birds.

Crows are extremely susceptible to infection with the exotic mosquito-borne West Nile virus, and have a high mortality rate from the disease. Other corvids, including Blue Jays and ravens are also affected, and the disease may cause illness in humans and horses. The virus, which originated from the Middle East, first appeared in the United States in 1999 in New York City. Following infection in 1999, crow populations in some areas of New York declined as much as 90%. Given the crow's high sensitivity to this virus, the appearance of dead crows may serve as an early indicator of the disease in an area.

Tree Swallow
Tachycineta bicolor

Family: Hirundinidae (Swallows)

Meaning of Scientific Name:
Tachycineta – derived from the Greek *tachy*, meaning fast, and *cine*, meaning motion.
bicolor – of two colors (Latin)

Tree Swallows in the Beaver Pond. April 15, 2011.

Diet: Eats insects while flying. Eats bayberry before migration and during winter.

Nest: In tree cavities (often old woodpecker holes), fence posts, holes in buildings, or bird boxes, usually 5 to 10 feet above ground, in open areas, usually near water. The entrance hole is normally 1½ inches in diameter and the nest is lined with grasses and feathers. In Massachusetts, lays eggs between mid-April and mid-June and has one brood per year. Nests are rarely parasitized by cowbirds. Tree Swallows compete for nest sites with European Starlings, House Sparrows, House Wrens, and Eastern Bluebirds.

History: The history of the Tree Swallow in our area closely parallels that of the Eastern Phoebe and the Eastern Kingbird. The Tree Swallow, which requires open areas for feeding, was common during the late 1800s and early 1900s when the land was mostly cleared and insects were in abundance. During the mid-1900s it was considered uncommon, probably due to the greater forest cover and the prevalence of DDT and other pesticides. The use of pesticides would have reduced the amount of food available to swallows. Also, the Tree Swallow bioaccumulates contaminants to a high degree, and pesticides and other contaminants in the environment may have affected the health and reproductive ability of this species. Currently, the Tree Swallow is a common summer resident in our area.

Since the 1920s, the Tree Swallow has been expanding its breeding range southward along the east coast. Previously, it did not breed south of Maryland. However, it is now known to nest regularly in many of the southern states, including Virginia, the Carolinas, Georgia, Alabama, Mississippi, and Texas.

Other Notes: Tree Swallows arrive at Den Rock's Beaver Pond by late March/early April, and are seen flying over the pond throughout spring and summer. They are normally present in small flocks and are constantly circling about, catching insects. By July and August they start assembling along the coast in preparation for migration, with most birds departing between August and October. Migratory flights occur during the day. Tree Swallows spend the winter along the United States coast from Virginia to Florida, and in Cuba and northern Central America.

BLACK-CAPPED CHICKADEE
Poecile atricapillus

Family: Paridae (Titmice)

Meaning of Scientific Name:
Poecile – from the Greek *poecil*, meaning variegated
atricapillus – derived from the Latin *ater* meaning black and *capillus* referring to hair on the head.

A Black-capped Chickadee inspecting a pine cone along the edge of Stirling Street by the Beaver Pond. March 11, 2010.

Diet: Insects, spiders, seeds and berries.

Nest: Excavates a hole in a dead, partially rotted tree or branch; also uses tree cavities of other birds and nest boxes. The nest cavity is typically 4 to 15 feet above ground, lined with soft fibers, and has an entrance hole approximately 1 inch in diameter. Being cavity nesters, and given the small size of the entrance hole, chickadees are rarely parasitized by Brown-headed Cowbirds. Eggs are laid between early May and mid-July in Massachusetts and one or two broods are raised per year.

History: The Black-capped Chickadee has been common in our area throughout known history and its distribution has not changed much over time. The chickadee can be seen regularly throughout Massachusetts during all seasons of the year. Given its familiar nature, the Black-capped Chickadee was designated the state bird of Massachusetts in 1941.

Other Notes: Black-capped Chickadees do not normally migrate and may be observed at Den Rock Park year round. They are often present in the pine trees along the western edge of the Beaver Pond at Stirling Street. During the non-breeding season (late summer/early fall through late winter) they occur in flocks, sometimes intermixed with other species such as Tufted Titmice, White-breasted Nuthatches, and Downy Woodpeckers. The male's sweet "Fee-bee" song is frequently heard in the park during late winter and early spring at the start of the breeding season.

TUFTED TITMOUSE
Baeolophus bicolor

Family: Paridae (Titmice)

Meaning of Scientific Name:
Baeolophus – from the Greek *bae*, meaning small, and *lophos* meaning crest
bicolor – of two colors (Latin)

Diet: Insects, spiders, seeds and berries. Acorns may constitute most of their diet from November to February.

Tufted Titmouse

Nest: Uses existing natural tree cavities or abandoned woodpecker holes 3 to 90 feet above ground; occasionally nests in bird boxes. Requires a nest hole of at least 1½ inches in diameter. Builds a cup nest of leaves, moss, bark strips, hair, and fur. In Massachusetts, eggs are laid during May and June with one brood raised per year. It is uncommon for cowbirds to parasitize their nests.

History: Traditionally a species of the southeastern states, the Tufted Titmouse only recently expanded its range north into New England, nesting for the first time in Massachusetts in 1958. Prior to 1934 it was reportedly observed only five times in Connecticut.

Possible explanations for its northward range expansion have included climate change, an increase in suburban winter bird feeders, and maturing forests in the Northeast.

Other Notes: The Tufted Titmouse's song "Peter Peter Peter Peter" or "Here Here Here Here" is commonly heard in Den Rock Park from late winter through spring. The titmouse may be observed in the oak forest or in residential areas near the edges of the park, but it is unlikely to be spotted in the Beaver Pond. It occurs year-round in the park and does not migrate.

WHITE-BREASTED NUTHATCH
Sitta carolinensis

Family: Sittidae (Nuthatches)

Meaning of Scientific Name:
Sitta – derived from *sitte*, a Greek word for nuthatch
carolinensis – of [North or South] Carolina

Diet: Insects and spiders. In the winter it eats many acorns and nuts. May cache food in bark crevices or on the underside of branches. Creeps headfirst down trunks.

Nest: Builds a bed of bark shreds, fur, hair, feathers, rootlets and grasses in an existing tree cavity (a natural cavity in a live tree is preferred, but it will also nest in dying or dead trees, abandoned woodpecker holes and bird houses). Requires a cavity at least 1½ inches in diameter but often uses larger holes. The nest cavity is typically 5 to 50 feet above ground. Prefers to nest in trees with a diameter at breast height of 12 inches. In Massachusetts eggs are laid from early April to May and one brood is raised per year. The nests are rarely parasitized by cowbirds.

White-breasted Nuthatch

History: The White-breasted Nuthatch has been a permanent resident in our area throughout known history. It is frequently observed in suburban areas and is a regular visitor at bird feeders.

Other Notes: Like the Tufted Titmouse, the White-breasted Nuthatch may be spotted in Den Rock's oak forest or in adjacent residential areas, but it is unlikely to be seen in the Beaver Pond. White-breasted Nuthatches do not normally migrate and may be observed year round.

EASTERN BLUEBIRD
Sialia sialis

Eastern Bluebird

Family: Turdidae (Bluebirds and Thrushes)

Meaning of Scientific Name: Derived from the Greek word *sialis*, meaning a kind of bird.

Diet: Insects and other invertebrates. Dependent on berries and seeds in the winter.

Nest: A loose cup of dried grasses and weeds in a tree cavity 5 to 20 feet above ground. Also uses nest boxes. Nest has an inside diameter of 2½ to 3 inches. Nests in open areas, beaver ponds, or forest edges. In Massachusetts, bluebirds lay eggs between early April and the first week of August, and usually have two (sometimes three) broods per year. On rare occasions nests may be parasitized by cowbirds, starlings or other bluebirds.

History: The Eastern Bluebird utilizes open habitats for feeding and nesting and requires perches, such as trees or posts, for foraging. The widespread clearing of land for agriculture during the 18th and 19th centuries expanded habitat favorable to this species. Traditionally bluebirds nested in old woodpecker holes in wooden fence posts and rails and in apple trees. They also nested in bird boxes put up by farmers, who welcomed these insect-eaters for protection against crop pests. The bluebird was considered common in southern New England during the mid-1800s but began declining by the late 1800s as farmlands disappeared and nest sites became scarce. With fewer and fewer nest sites available, the bluebird experienced intense competition for nest cavities with other birds, especially the aggressive non-native European Starling and House Sparrow. As a result, bluebird populations in the Northeast declined by approximately 90 percent. Other factors contributing to the bluebird's decline included the use of metal instead of wooden fence posts, severe winters, and the widespread use of pesticides, especially DDT. Pesticides decreased the food source available to bluebirds, and DDT exposure may have reduced the hatchability of their eggs.

An Eastern Bluebird in the Beaver Pond. July 11, 2010.

Bluebird populations began to rebound beginning in the 1970s with the establishment of bluebird nest box programs across the country.

The spread of the beaver has also aided bluebirds by creating habitats with dead standing trees, providing many nesting sites. The banning of DDT in 1972 contributed to the bluebird's recovery.

Other Notes: The Eastern Bluebird is occasionally observed on dead standing trees in the Beaver Pond during spring and summer. The bluebird is migratory, flying during the day. It arrives in Massachusetts from mid-March through April. Fall migration takes place during October. The bluebird overwinters in the southeastern United States, to as far north as southern New England. Some remain in Massachusetts during the winter.

AMERICAN ROBIN
Turdus migratorius

Family: Turdidae (Bluebirds and Thrushes)

Meaning of Scientific Name:
Turdus – thrush (Latin)
migratorius – wanderer (Latin)

Diet: Earthworms and insects during spring and summer; mostly fruit/berries during fall and winter.

Nest: Constructed of grasses with a middle layer of mud. They are typically located on a horizontal limb 5 to 30 feet above ground. White Pine, maple, and apple trees are most commonly used for nesting. The nests have an outside diameter of 6½ inches (inside diameter of 4 inches). In Massachusetts, eggs are laid between mid-April and late July and two or three broods are raised per year. Robin nests are rarely parasitized by cowbirds. Robins are known to puncture cowbird eggs and throw them out of their nests.

American Robin

History: The American Robin has been a common bird in New England throughout the known past. Many were hunted and trapped for food and for sport up until the mid-1800s. The Migratory Bird Treaty Act currently protects this songbird from hunting.

During the 1950s, American Robins were killed in large numbers from the spraying of DDT to control the spread of beetles carrying Dutch Elm Disease. Massive die-offs of robins were documented in studies conducted at Michigan State University, the

University of Wisconsin at Madison, and Hanover, New Hampshire following DDT spray events. Robins feed on earthworms, which are insensitive to DDT and concentrate it in their tissues at levels as high as 5 times those in the surrounding soil. DDT has since been banned and American Robins are currently one of the most abundant breeding birds in the state.

Other Notes: During spring and summer American Robins may be seen and heard at various locations in Den Rock Park, including the Beaver Pond, edges of the oak forest, and by the Shawsheen River. Most robins that breed in Canada and the northern United States are migratory and overwinter in the southern United States and Mexico. Migration occurs during the day. Migrating robins generally arrive in Massachusetts during March and April. Peak fall migration in our area takes place during late October. Many robins overwinter in Massachusetts, although during severe winters they will fly to more hospitable locations. During fall and winter, robins forage in large roving flocks and may occasionally be observed feeding on berries by the Shawsheen River.

EUROPEAN STARLING
Sturnus vulgaris

Family: Sturnidae (Starlings)

Meaning of Scientific Name:
Sturnus – starling (Latin)
vulgaris – common (Latin)

Diet: Insects, spiders, earthworms, salamanders, snails, seeds, fruits, cultivated grains and garbage.

Nest: In the hole of a tree or building 10 to 30 feet above ground. Requires a cavity at least 1½ inches in diameter.

A starling in the Beaver Pond. March 11, 2012.

Lines the nest with dead leaves and grasses. In Massachusetts starlings lay eggs from early April to July. They have one or two broods per year. Nests are commonly parasitized by other starlings and rarely by Brown-headed Cowbirds.

European Starling

History: Starlings were introduced to New York City in the early 1890s from Europe. They were released by a group known as the American Acclimatization Society. Other releases occurred in the United States previous to that time, but were unsuccessful.

Acclimatization societies were formed during the mid- to late 1800s as part of an Acclimatization Movement that originated in France. These societies were created with the primary purpose of introducing foreign plants and animals and helping such species become naturalized or "acclimatized" to their new environment. Acclimatization societies were established in France and Great Britain, and became most prevalent in French and British colonies in places such as Australia, New Zealand, Algeria, Reunion, and Martinique. Acclimatization societies also formed in New York City, Cincinnati and other locations in the United States.

Members of these societies included naturalists and wealthy emigrants from Europe. They imported and released species, mostly from Europe, for a number of reasons: for food, to control pests, to provide game for hunters, to beautify their gardens and landscapes, to create an environment similar to their European homelands, and/or for other economic or cultural purposes. Acclimatization society members and others who deliberately released non-native species into the wild lacked an understanding of ecology and were unaware of the potential damage that could be caused by their actions. Some of the foreign species that were introduced, such as the European Starling, became invasive in their new environments. Invasive species behave like invaders—rapidly spreading across a landscape, multiplying and consuming resources at the expense of native populations, and often causing declines in or in some cases, extinctions, of resident species as well as environmental degradation. Most acclimatization societies disappeared by the late 1800s, by which time the consequences of their actions started to become apparent.

In addition to being released in the United States, European Starlings were also successfully introduced to South Africa, New Zealand, and Australia. Today the European Starling is considered by the Invasive Species Specialist Group to be one of the world's 100 worst invasive alien species.

Progeny of the starlings introduced to New York City became common in Massachusetts by the 1920s. They have since spread throughout the United States and into southern and central Canada and northern Mexico. Starlings compete aggressively for nesting sites with other birds, and are believed to have contributed to the decline of native cavity nesters, including the Eastern Bluebird.

Considered major pests in the United States, starlings consume animal feed in livestock feedlots, and cause damage to sprouting wheat and other crops. They may spread diseases between livestock in different feedlots, and they are considered a nuisance and/or hazard when they roost in urban areas or near airports. From late summer through winter, starlings forage in large flocks, and at night roost communally in aggregations that may contain over a million birds.

Being a non-native, invasive species, the starling is not protected by the Migratory Bird Treaty Act. Therefore, it may be killed without a federal permit. A commercially available pesticide called

Starlicide Complete is used to destroy starlings and blackbirds in livestock feedlots and poultry operations. If starling damage cannot be controlled using *Starlicide Complete*, firearms, or other means, USDA APHIS Wildlife Services personnel may be contacted for assistance. USDA personnel may administer a more potent pesticide product, known as *Starlicide Technical* or DRC-1339, or may utilize other methods to destroy or disperse starlings and minimize crop damage.

During 2010 and 2011, USDA APHIS Wildlife Services personnel killed approximately 1.5 to 2.5 million starlings per year. More starlings were killed by USDA personnel during these years than any other species of bird, mammal or reptile. Most of these birds (approximately 90 percent) were poisoned in livestock feedlots using DRC-1339.

Ironically, in the United Kingdom where the starling is considered native, it is designated as a "red list" (highest concern) species on the region's list of Birds of Conservation Concern. In Great Britain, where starlings occur mostly on farmland (the predominant land type there), the species has declined by nearly 70% since the early 1960s. The decline is believed to be due to a reduction in the starling's food supply (soil invertebrates and grains), which is possibly caused by a decrease in land area used for pasture (where soil invertebrates are most abundant); a decrease in the number of cattle (which stir up and expose invertebrate food for the starling, and which are fed grains that the starling consumes); a tendency to keep cattle indoors (where the starling has less access to cattle feed); and an increase in the use of insecticides, anthelmintics, and fertilizers (which adversely affect the availability of invertebrate food).

Other Notes: European Starlings occur year-round in Massachusetts. At Den Rock Park, starlings are most frequently observed during spring and summer on trees in the Beaver Pond. Unlike Red-winged Blackbirds or Common Grackles, which take up seasonal residence in the Beaver Pond, starlings typically appear on a somewhat irregular basis. A flock of starlings may be seen for a few days in the pond and then may not be spotted again at Den Rock for weeks or months.

In Massachusetts, starlings may be legally hunted by licensed hunters throughout the year with no bag limits.

Song Sparrow
Melospiza melodia

Family: Emberizidae (Towhees, Sparrows, and Allies)

Meaning of Scientific Name:
Melospiza – derived from the Greek *melos*, meaning song, and *spiza*, meaning finch
melodia – Greek and Latin for "pleasant song"

Diet: Seeds, insects, and some berries.

A Song Sparrow on a stump in the Beaver Pond. April 1, 2010.

Nest: Builds a nest of mostly grasses with some bark strands and leaves. The nest has an inside diameter of 2¼ inches and is located among shrubs or high weeds, on the ground or up to 4 feet above ground. Along with the Yellow Warbler, the Song Sparrow is the most frequent cowbird host. In Massachusetts, Song Sparrows lay eggs between late April and late July and have two or three broods per year.

History: Song Sparrows have been reported to be common summer residents in Massachusetts throughout known history.

Other Notes: Song Sparrows may be observed throughout the year at Den Rock Park and are often seen during spring singing from prominent perches in the Beaver Pond. Most Song Sparrows are migratory, although some remain in Massachusetts during the winter. Song Sparrows generally arrive in Massachusetts during late March/early April. They begin their migration south during September and October, overwintering in the southern United States.

NORTHERN CARDINAL
Cardinalis cardinalis

Family: Cardinalidae (Cardinals)

Meaning of Scientific Name:
Cardinalis – scarlet or cardinal red, as in the color of a cardinal's robe.

Diet: Insects, spiders, wild fruits and berries, weed seeds.

Northern Cardinal

Nest: A loosely assembled cup nest of twigs, vines, weeds, grass, bark, and leaves, which is lined with fine grasses, rootlets, and hair. The nest has an outside diameter of 5⅜ inches and is found in dense thickets and shrubs, usually less than 10 feet above ground. In Massachusetts, eggs are laid between late April and late June. Typically two or three broods are raised per year. Cardinal nests are commonly parasitized by Brown-headed Cowbirds.

History: Although Northern Cardinals are now one of our most common suburban birds, they only recently expanded their range northward into New England. The cardinal was traditionally a bird of the southeastern United States. The first confirmed nesting record for the Northern Cardinal in Massachusetts was in 1961, and by 1970, nesting birds were observed throughout the state. Possible explanations for the northward range expansion have included suburbanization and other development, which have created habitat favorable to the cardinal, climate change, and increased food availability during winter from backyard bird feeders.

During the 1800s, cardinals were popular as caged birds. They were trapped in the southeastern states and imported to the north for sale as pets. This practice was ended by the Migratory Bird Treaty Act of 1918, which prohibited the capture, market sale and possession of cardinals and other native songbirds.[5]

A male Northern Cardinal on the guard rail along the edge of Stirling Street by the Beaver Pond. March 11, 2010.

Other Notes: Northern Cardinals may be observed and heard along edges of the park bordering suburban areas. They are year-round residents and are not known to migrate.

---

[5] Earlier federal legislation was passed to protect native birds but was considered inadequate due to loopholes and poor enforcement (i.e., the Lacey Act of 1900) or constitutional weakness (i.e., the Weeks-McLean Act of 1913).

Red-winged Blackbird
Agelaius phoeniceus

Family: Icteridae (Blackbirds, Orioles and Allies)

Meaning of Scientific Name:
Agelaius – from the Greek *agelaios* meaning flocking
phoeniceus – Purple-red (Latin), in reference to a dye from Phoenicia (an ancient civilization occupying what is now Israel, Palestinian territories, Lebanon, and western Jordan). The Phoenicians were known for a purple dye derived from *Murex* snails.

Diet: Primarily insects during breeding season, and mostly seeds during fall and winter.

Nest: A cup nest of woven grasses, cattails or other marsh vegetation, in shrubs or among reeds 3 to 8 feet high, near water. The nest has an inside diameter of approximately 3 inches and may contain a middle layer of mud. It is lined with fine grasses. The birds nest in loose colonies. In Massachusetts, eggs are laid between mid-May and mid-June. Two or three broods are raised per year. Nests are frequently parasitized by cowbirds.

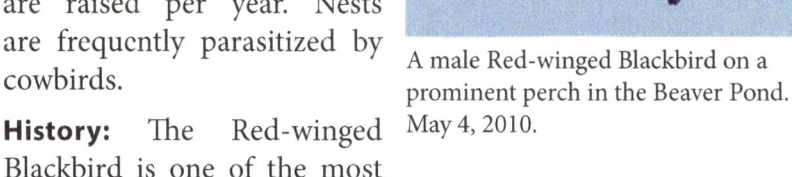

A male Red-winged Blackbird on a prominent perch in the Beaver Pond. May 4, 2010.

History: The Red-winged Blackbird is one of the most abundant birds in North America. It has been common and abundant in Massachusetts throughout the historic period. Since colonial times, blackbirds have been considered a pest of crops. During the 17th and 18th centuries various towns in Massachusetts offered bounties for blackbirds.

Traditionally, the Red-winged Blackbird nested in wetlands, as it does today. However, it is estimated that more than half of the wetlands that existed in the contiguous United States prior to the 1600s have been filled. In several Midwestern states, including Iowa, Missouri, and Illinois, wetlands were almost completely converted to croplands. Today, the Red-winged Blackbird is known to nest in both wetland and upland habitats. In the Midwest where wetlands are scarce it nests primarily in upland areas.

During its non-breeding season (fall and winter), when the Red-winged Blackbird consumes primarily plant material, it is considered a major agricultural pest. Impacted crops include corn, sunflower, and rice.

Although protected by the Migratory Bird Treaty Act, federal regulations permit the killing of Red-winged Blackbirds (as well as other blackbirds, cowbirds, grackles, crows, and magpies)[6] without a federal permit if they are causing or about to cause harm to ornamental or shade trees, agricultural crops, livestock, or wildlife, or if they are concentrated in large numbers so as to constitute a health hazard or other nuisance. From 1974 to 1992, Red-winged Blackbirds depredating crops were commonly killed in large numbers using the surfactant PA-14, a chemical that was registered by the U.S. Environmental Protection Agency (EPA) for lethal control of blackbirds and starlings. PA-14 was sprayed, either aerially or using ground sprinklers, on birds at roosts. Surfactants such as PA-14 cause feathers to lose their ability to repel water. When the feathers get wet, they become saturated and no longer provide insulation. The birds are unable to stay warm and die of hypothermia.

---

[6] The Rusty Blackbird was recently excluded from this list due to long-term declines. However, it often flocks with more common blackbird species, making it difficult to prevent mortalities when lethal control is used for other blackbirds.

The use of PA-14 was discontinued in 1992 after the EPA requested additional data on the product (required for continued registration), which would have been costly to provide.

Currently DRC-1339 is used for lethal control of blackbirds. DRC-1339 is a restricted use pesticide that may be applied only by USDA APHIS Wildlife Services personnel or by persons under their direct supervision. It is normally used when agricultural damage caused by blackbirds cannot be adequately controlled using commercially available pesticides or by other available means such as shooting, trapping, repellents, exploders, frightening agents or other non-lethal or lethal methods. DRC-1339 is a slow-acting poison used in bait that causes organ failure over a period of 1 to 3 days. Because DRC-1339 is slow-acting, sometimes birds will fly several miles after being poisoned. On rare occasions, poisoned birds will fly into suburban areas—dropping dead by the hundreds or thousands—to the bewilderment of residents.

During 2009 through 2011, between 500,000 and 1 million Red-winged Blackbirds were killed each year by USDA APHIS Wildlife Services personnel using DRC-1339. More than 95% of these birds were killed in Louisiana and Texas, where overwintering blackbirds cause substantial damage to rice fields.

Red-winged Blackbirds are considered the number one pest of sunflower crops, which are grown primarily in North and South Dakota. Damage occurs during fall migration. The sunflower fields most affected are those located closest to blackbird roosting areas, which typically consist of cattail marshes. Historically, these marshes contained open water and were only sparsely vegetated. However, during the 1940s, the non-native Narrow-leaved Cattail was inadvertently introduced. It cross-pollinated with the native Common Cattail producing a hybrid, which rapidly invaded wetlands. The hybrid cattail grew into dense stands in the wetlands it colonized, providing ideal habitat for Red-winged Blackbirds for nesting and roosting.

During the past 20 years, USDA APHIS Wildlife Services has operated a Cattail Management Program in North and South Dakota as a means of reducing blackbird damage to sunflower crops. Under this program sunflower growers may apply to have wetlands located near their fields sprayed with herbicide in order to reduce favorable habitat for blackbirds. In North Dakota, large numbers of blackbirds are also dispersed using pyrotechnics and firearms.

Other Notes: The Red-winged Blackbird is a very common seasonal resident of Den Rock's Beaver Pond. It is usually present in the pond by the second week in March and may be regularly seen through late July. The males are very conspicuous and easily observed. They frequently occur in mixed flocks with grackles, and their song "konk-la-ree" is often heard. The females have brown-streaked, sparrow-like coloration and are often secretive and difficult to spot.

Most populations of Red-winged Blackbirds that breed in Canada and the northern United States overwinter in the southern United States. On the east coast, the blackbird's wintering range extends as far north as southern Nova Scotia. However, the Red-winged Blackbird is considered uncommon during winter in Massachusetts and other areas to the north.

Red-winged Blackbirds arrive in Massachusetts between late February and early April. Prior to fall migration, they gather in huge flocks, with most departing for their southern wintering grounds between late August and early November. Migration occurs during the day.

COMMON GRACKLE
Quiscalus quiscula

Family: Icteridae (Blackbirds, Orioles and Allies)

Meaning of Scientific Name:
Origin is unknown. Possibly derived from the Latin *quiscalis*, meaning quail; the Spanish word *quisquilla*, meaning a quibble; or the Latin word *quisquiliae* for rubbish or refuse.

Diet: Insects, weed seeds, grains, fruit, acorns, minnows, small crayfish, rodents, and birds.

Nest: Constructs a nest of grasses and mud on horizontal branches 3 to 30 feet high. The nest has an outside diameter of approximately 7 to 9 inches (inside diameter of 4 inches) and is often located in an evergreen tree. Grackles may also nest in natural cavities or ledges. Many pairs of birds may nest in the vicinity of one another. In Massachusetts, eggs are laid between early May and early June. Grackles have one brood per year and are rarely parasitized by cowbirds.

A Common Grackle on a log in the Beaver Pond. April 15, 2011.

History: Like the Red-winged Blackbird, the Common Grackle has been considered a pest of crops since colonial times. As agriculture spread across the country, the grackle expanded its range westward. Previously, the Common Grackle was considered rare in the western portion of the country. It now breeds in several western states including Colorado, Montana, and Idaho. Since the mid-20th century it has been observed along the west coast, where it is believed to begin breeding soon.

The Common Grackle is a major agricultural pest in the United States, causing damage to corn, rice, and sunflower crops. It may also consume grain in livestock feedlots. The grackle feeds in large flocks during its non-breeding season (late summer through winter). It often flocks with other species including Red-winged Blackbirds, European Starlings, and Brown-headed Cowbirds. From late summer through winter, Common Grackles assemble during the evening in large numbers at roosting areas in trees where they spend the night. A given roost may contain over a million birds. Prior to settling for the night at the roost, the birds typically begin flocking in nearby trees, an activity known as "staging."

A Common Grackle fledgling in the Beaver Pond. The nest was located in a cavity in a dead tree along the edge of the pond. May 30, 2010.

When roosting areas are located near areas used by people they are usually considered a nuisance due to the noise and the droppings that accumulate on the ground. When grackles, other blackbirds, or starlings occupy roosts for three or more years, the roosts often become infected with the fungus that causes histoplasmosis (a respiratory disease that is contracted by inhaling the fungal spores). The fungus commonly occurs in areas with accumulated bird or bat droppings. Although the infection causes no symptoms in most people, infants and people with compromised immune systems may become severely ill from it.

Common Grackles are protected under the Migratory Bird Treaty Act, which prohibits the killing, possession, and transport of these birds (and their feathers, nests, and eggs) without a federal permit. However, federal regulations (50 CFR 21.43) allow the killing of grackles without a permit if they are "committing or about to commit depredations on ornamental or shade trees, agricultural crops, livestock, or wildlife, or when concentrated in such numbers and manner that they are a health hazard or other nuisance..."

From 1974 to 1992 the surfactant PA-14 was used to kill overwintering Common Grackles, European Starlings, Red-winged Blackbirds, and Brown-headed Cowbirds that were considered a threat to crops or otherwise considered a nuisance. The surfactant, which was sprayed on birds at roosts, affected the ability of the feathers to shed water, causing the birds to die of hypothermia. An estimated 2 million birds were killed per year using this method; approximately half of these were Common Grackles. PA-14 was used primarily in Kentucky and Tennessee.

The pesticide DRC-1339 is now commonly used for lethal control of Common Grackles when damage cannot be adequately controlled using other methods. Approximately 100,000 Common Grackles were killed per year by USDA APHIS Wildlife Services personnel using this method during 2009 and 2010; about 40,000 were killed during 2011. Most of these grackles were killed in the rice-producing states of Louisiana and Texas. The total number of grackles killed in the United States during these years is unknown, as reporting requirements were not mandated for all depredation control actions until 2011.[7]

According to National Audubon Society estimates, numbers of Common Grackles in North America have declined by approximately 60% over the past 40 years. The cause for the decline is not well understood. Although Red-winged Blackbirds and Common Grackles have life histories that are much alike, a similar decline has not been identified for Red-winged Blackbirds.

Despite their decline, Common Grackles are still common and abundant birds in the United States.

---

[7] Since January 2011, the U.S. Fish and Wildlife Service has required reporting of all control actions taken under the *Depredation order for blackbirds, cowbirds, grackles, crows and magpies* (50 CFR 21.43). Data on the total number of grackles killed in 2011 and 2012 under the depredation order are not available, as outreach efforts still need to be conducted to ensure individuals and agencies are aware of the new reporting requirement.

Other Notes: Grackles can be regularly seen at the Beaver Pond during spring and summer, often in the company of male Red-winged Blackbirds. They are usually present in the Beaver Pond by the second week of March.

Common Grackles generally overwinter in the southern United States, although some may overwinter as far north as southern New Hampshire and Vermont, dependent on weather. Migration occurs during the day. The first spring migrants usually arrive in Massachusetts during late February and early March. Peak fall migration occurs during late October/early November.

Each fall Common Grackles roost at night in huge numbers at a location in Methuen known as Peat Meadow. Peat Meadow is located on private property just west of Interstate 93. It consists mostly of wetland and is bisected by a transmission line corridor. As many as a million Common Grackles may be observed roosting at this location before flying south for the winter. Along with the grackles, thousands of Red-winged Blackbirds, thousands of American Robins, and hundreds of Rusty Blackbirds have been observed roosting here. Given the high concentrations of birds that use this area, Peat Meadow has been designated as an Important Bird Area in Massachusetts.

During spring migration the grackles and other blackbirds once again occupy roosts at Peat Meadow. However, their populations tend to be much smaller at this time, as many die from the rigors of migration and winter, and, to some extent, from agricultural pest control measures.

Brown-headed Cowbird
Molothrus ater

Family: Icteridae (Blackbirds, Orioles and Allies)

Meaning of Scientific Name:
Molothrus – meaning parasite or greedy person (Greek)
ater – dead-black (Latin)

Diet: Forages on the ground eating grain, grass, weed seeds, and insects.

Nest: Does not build a nest; lays its eggs in the nests of other birds (considered a brood parasite). In Massachusetts, eggs are laid between mid-May and early July. As many as 40 eggs may be laid per season (nearly one egg per day), with approximately 3 percent surviving to adulthood. Usually the cowbird lays one egg in each nest that it parasitizes and removes one egg of the host bird. Cowbirds don't normally parasitize cavity nesting birds or birds much larger than themselves.

A male Brown-headed Cowbird flying off of a perch in the Beaver Pond. April 11, 2010.

History: Historically, the Brown-headed Cowbird was a bird of the Great Plains. It lived in association with bison and was once known as the "buffalo bird." The range of the Brown-headed Cowbird more or less corresponded with that of the plains bison.

The bison is a nonterritorial roaming animal. Most bison are believed to have been migratory, undergoing seasonal movements of perhaps a few hundred miles. The cowbird followed the roaming herds of bison, feeding on insects stirred up by these large animals.

Also, the grazing action of the bison reduced the amount of vegetation in the ground cover, making it easier for the cowbird to locate insects and seeds.

Brown-headed Cowbirds are obligate brood parasites. They never build nests of their own and always lay their eggs in the nests of other bird species (with the host bird taking full responsibility for the care of the cowbird young). Because of this reproductive strategy, the cowbird never needed to stay put during its breeding season to tend a nest and offspring—to do so would have caused the cowbird to separate from the bison herd, making it much harder to obtain food. Instead, over the course of its breeding period, the cowbird laid its eggs in the nests of other birds that the bison passed by during their wanderings.

It is believed that the range of the bison (and therefore that of most Brown-headed Cowbirds) was restricted to the Great Plains because of hunting pressures from Native Americans. During the 1600s, Native American populations were decimated from diseases brought over by Europeans. Following declines in native people, numbers of bison surged. The bison expanded its range to the east and west. Bison were observed for the first time in the eastern United States during the late 1600s, often in lands formerly occupied by Native Americans. To the west, the bison spread out as far as California. The Brown-headed Cowbird expanded its range to the east and west as well.

As European settlers cleared forests in the east and brought in cattle, the Brown-headed Cowbird further expanded its range in the east and began feeding alongside cattle. Meanwhile the bison that had ventured into the east were rapidly killed by hunters, and were extirpated by 1680 in Maryland, by 1772 in Virginia, by 1775 in the Carolinas, and by 1770 in Georgia. With the westward movement of settlers in the 1800s, the bison of the plains were heavily hunted and the prairie habitat of the bison came to be home to increasing numbers of cattle.

In the early 1800s, the plains bison were estimated to number around 30 million. By the late 1800s, they were nearly exterminated in the wild. The bison were killed by market hunters—mostly for their hides; they were shot by hunters such as "Buffalo Bill" Cody to provide meat to workers laying the tracks for the Kansas Pacific Railway; they were killed by railroad companies to prevent collisions with trains; and they were killed for sport—in buffalo hunting contests, and by tourists from windows of trains. The killing of the bison was also seen by some as a way to defeat the Native Americans and gain control of the West, as the Native American tribes of the plains were dependent on the bison for their sustenance and way of life, having lived alongside the bison for thousands of years.

With the demise of the bison and the spread of cattle, the "buffalo bird" became a bird of agricultural areas and began to be known as the "cow blackbird" or "cowbird." Today Brown-headed Cowbirds may be found throughout most of North America, often in association with cattle and other ungulates. They typically forage in open habitats, such as pastures, fields, and suburban areas, and are most likely to lay their eggs in nests located near forest edges.

During pre-colonial times the cowbird parasitized the nests of an estimated 50 species of birds. Now Brown-headed Cowbirds are known to successfully parasitize the nests of 144 species. More species have become accessible to the cowbird due to the fragmentation of forests and the subsequent increase in "edge" habitat. The nests of birds that breed in forest interiors were previously out of limits to the cowbird, as cowbirds do not normally venture deep into forests. However, as forested areas have become bisected by roads and transmission line corridors and carved up into increasingly smaller lots as a result of development, more and more "forest interiors" are falling within the habitat limits of the breeding cowbird.

Brood parasitism by Brown-headed Cowbirds is believed to be contributing to the decline of forest-breeding neotropical migratory songbirds. Such birds breed in temperate forests of North America and winter in Central and South America. Neotropical migratory songbirds that breed in forest interiors, such as wood warblers, thrushes, and vireos, did not evolve in the presence of cowbirds and so have few defenses against them. Also, they migrate long distances so they tend to lay only one clutch of eggs per season, and therefore have only one opportunity per year to successfully raise young. The cowbird eggs typically hatch before the eggs of the host bird and the cowbird nestlings tend to be larger, grow faster, and receive more food than the host's own young. Consequently, birds parasitized by the cowbird fledge fewer young of their own.

Cowbird parasitism is especially problematic when it affects species such as the Kirtland's Warbler, Black-capped Vireo, and Least Bell's Vireo, which are already rare due to habitat loss and/or limited availability of suitable habitat. As part of the management of these federally-endangered species, Brown-headed Cowbirds are trapped in the breeding areas of these rare birds to minimize rates of parasitism. Brown-headed Cowbirds have been trapped and euthanized in the breeding areas of the Kirtland's Warbler in Michigan every year since 1972. The Kirtland's Warbler breeds only within a restricted habitat type (young Jack Pine forest) in restricted areas of Michigan, Wisconsin, and Ontario, and nowhere else in the world. Land development, fire suppression policies and cowbird parasitism have contributed to this warbler's decline. Without the on-going cowbird trapping program, the Kirtland's Warbler would not be able to reproduce at a rate high enough to offset its mortality rate and would soon go extinct.

Other Notes: Although brood parasitism has been observed in a number of bird taxa, including many waterfowl, obligate brood parasitism is believed to be relatively rare, occurring in only 1% of all bird species. Besides the Brown-headed Cowbird, known obligate brood parasites include four other species of cowbirds (found in the Americas), the Black-headed Duck (found in South America), approximately 50 species of cuckoos (family Cuculidae) (found mostly in the Old World, with three obligate brood parasites occurring in Central and South America), 17 species of honeyguides (family Indicatoridae) (found in Africa and Asia), and two genera of finches from Africa.

Like other blackbirds, Brown-headed Cowbirds are considered major agricultural pests. Along with Red-winged Blackbirds and Common Grackles, they cause extensive damage to newly planted and ripening rice in Louisiana, Texas, Arkansas, Missouri, and California. Although the Brown-headed Cowbird is protected under the Migratory Bird Treaty Act, federal regulations permit the killing of cowbirds without a permit when they are "found committing or about to commit depredations upon ornamental or shade trees, agricultural crops, livestock, or wildlife, or when concentrated in such numbers and manner as to constitute a health hazard or other nuisance."

Farms may employ various methods to control damage from cowbirds, such as the use of repellents or exploders. However, if available methods prove insufficient, the USDA may provide assistance. During 2009 through 2011, approximately one million Brown-headed Cowbirds were killed each year by USDA APHIS Wildlife Services personnel. Almost all of these birds were poisoned in Louisiana and Texas using the avian poison DRC-1339.

Brown-headed Cowbirds are considered short-distance migrants, with migration occurring during the day. Most cowbirds spend the winter in the middle and southern states, while a small number occur year-round in Massachusetts. Spring migrants usually arrive in Massachusetts during March. Fall migration takes place from September through November. During the fall, cowbirds may often be seen in mixed flocks foraging with other blackbirds and starlings.

Brown-headed Cowbirds are most easily observed at Den Rock Park from late March through mid-April. During this time, the males are often seen singing from high conspicuous perches in the Beaver Pond. The species at Den Rock that are most likely to be parasitized by the cowbird are the Song Sparrow, Northern Cardinal, Eastern Phoebe, and Red-winged Blackbird. The Eastern Kingbird is also often parasitized by the cowbird, although unsuccessfully.

House Sparrow
Passer domesticus

Family: Passeridae (Old World Sparrows)

Meaning of Scientific Name:
Passer – sparrow (Latin)
domesticus – from the house, domestic (Latin)

Diet: Cereal grains (including waste grain), weed seeds, insects, spiders, small fruit, garbage.

Nest: Constructs a somewhat spherical nest of grasses, leaves, and twigs, with an opening on one side. The nest has an outside diameter of 10 to 30 inches, and is built in protected areas of buildings or in cavities of trees, 10 to 30 feet above ground. The House Sparrow uses the nest in spring and summer for raising young, and during the fall and winter for resting and roosting. The same nest site is often used for life. In Massachusetts, eggs are laid between February and September and two or three broods are raised per year. House Sparrow nests are rarely parasitized by Brown-headed Cowbirds.

Male House Sparrow in non-breeding plumage.

History: The House Sparrow was first successfully introduced to the United States from Europe in the 1850s. By the turn of the century it was one of the most abundant bird species in the country, with populations peaking between 1890 and 1915. It thrived in urban areas, feeding on grain given to horses, as well as undigested grain in the manure. The House Sparrow has since decreased in number with the substitution of the automobile for the horse and the decline in agriculture.

Other Notes: House Sparrows are commonly seen along the western edge of the Beaver Pond. They are year-round residents and have been observed nesting in cavities in trees and stumps in the pond.

The House Sparrow is known to aggressively take over nests of other birds, especially bluebirds and swallows, and destroy existing eggs and nestlings. They may also kill the adult nesting birds. The House Sparrow is not protected under the Migratory Bird Treaty Act because it is not a native species. It is considered invasive and may be legally hunted in Massachusetts by licensed hunters year round with no bag limits.

In Europe, where the House Sparrow is considered native, it has experienced substantial declines. Changes in farming practices, including the increased use of pesticides and the improved management and storage of grain, are probably responsible for the decline of House Sparrows in agricultural areas. In urban areas, reasons for recent declines are not well understood. The House Sparrow is categorized as a "Red List" (highest concern) species on the United Kingdom's list of Birds of Conservation Concern. In addition, the House Sparrow is included on the International Union for Conservation of Nature (IUCN)'s Red List of Threatened Species. However, given its extensive range and large population size worldwide, the IUCN classifies it as a Red List species of "Least Concern."

A House Sparrow on a stump in the Beaver Pond. July 20, 2011.

Appendix A: Bird and Mammal Species Extirpated from Massachusetts since the Beginning of the Colonial Period

Birds

Species	Notes	Sources
Sandhill Crane *(Grus canadensis)*	Extirpated. Was reportedly observed in Massachusetts during the early colonial period. May have bred along the eastern coast from Florida to New England. In 2007 was observed breeding in Massachusetts. Has been regularly observed in Massachusetts during the breeding season since then.	5, 7, 9
Trumpeter Swan *(Cygnus buccinator)*	Extirpated. Formerly migrated from Long Island Sound and the mouth of the Hudson River to the Hudson Bay area. Reportedly passed through New England in migration. Believed to have occurred in Massachusetts around 1700 and before.	5, 7
Great Auk *(Pinguinus impennis)*	Wintering range included coastal Massachusetts. Extinct around 1844. Last record in Massachusetts during the 1700s.	2, 4, 5, 8
Whooping Crane *(Grus americana)*	Extirpated. Formerly ranged across the greater part of North America. Along the eastern coastline, it migrated from Florida to New England or further north. Believed to have appeared in Massachusetts during migration. In 1833 it was described as a rare but regular visitor.	5, 7
Wild Turkey *(Meleagris gallopavo)*	Extirpated around 1851. Reintroduced in 1972 and 1973.	10

APPENDIX A: SPECIES EXTIRPATED FROM MASSACHUSETTS

Species	Notes	Sources
Labrador Duck (*Camptorhynchus labradorius*)	Wintering range included coastal Massachusetts. Extinct around 1875.	2, 4, 5, 8
Dickcissel (*Spiza americana*)	Extirpated. Last nesting record in Massachusetts in 1877.	2
Passenger Pigeon (*Ectopistes migratorius*)	Formerly considered the most abundant bird species in North America. Extinct in 1914. Last record in Massachusetts in 1894.	2, 4, 8
Common Loon (*Gavia immer*)	Extirpated in the late 19th century. Since 1975 has been nesting again in Massachusetts.	15
Bald Eagle (*Haliaeetus leucocephalus*)	Extirpated in 1910 due to persecution and loss of habitat. Reintroduced during the 1980s.	14, 17
Eskimo Curlew (*Numenius borealis*)	Extinct. Formerly passed through coastal Massachusetts during migration. Last record in 1963 in Barbados. Last record in Massachusetts In 1913.	2, 4, 5
Heath Hen (*Tympanuchus cupido cupido*)*	Formerly occurred from Massachusetts to Virginia. Now extinct. Last record 1932 in Martha's Vineyard.	2, 4, 8
Peregrine Falcon (*Falco peregrinus*)	Extirpated in 1955 as a result of DDT. Reintroduced during the 1970s and 1980s.	14, 16
Loggerhead Shrike (*Lanius luduvicianus*)	Extirpated. Last nesting record in Massachusetts in 1971.	2
Bicknell's Thrush (*Catharus bicknelli*)	Extirpated. Formerly nested on Mt. Greylock. Last nesting record in Massachusetts in 1972.	1, 2
Olive-sided Flycatcher (*Contopus cooperi*)	Extirpated. Last nesting record in Massachusetts in 1991.	2

* A subspecies of the Greater Prairie-chicken

Mammals

Species	Notes	Sources
Wapiti (Elk) *(Cervus elaphus)*	Extirpated. Formerly occurred infrequently in western Massachusetts. Last record around 1732.	13
Beaver *(Castor canadensis)*	Extirpated around 1750. Observed in Massachusetts again in 1928. Additional beaver introduced from New York in 1932.	11
Fisher *(Martes pennant)*	Extirpated in the early 1800s. Has recently returned to the state.	12
Wolverine *(Gulo gulo)*	Extirpated. Formerly in western Massachusetts. Last record around 1835.	13
Wolf *(Canis lupis)*	Extirpated around 1840.	13
Mountain Lion *(Puma concolor)*	Extirpated. Last record around 1858.	13
American Marten *(Martes americana)*	Extirpated. Formerly in central and western Massachusetts. Last record 1880.	13
Canadian Lynx *(Lynx canadensis)*	Extirpated. Formerly in Hampshire and Worcester counties. Last record around 1885.	13
Sea Mink *(Neovison macrodon)*	Formerly in coastal Massachusetts. Extinct by around 1900.	3, 13
Indiana Bat *(Myotis sodalis)*	Probably extirpated (last record 1939).	13

Notes: Black Bear *(Ursus americanus)* and Moose *(Alces alces)* were virtually exterminated in Massachusetts as well; however stragglers were occasionally spotted in the state so these species were not considered truly extirpated (3, 6).

Sources:

1. Atwood, Jonathan L., Rimmer, Christopher C., Mcfarland, Kent J., Tsai, Sophia H., and Nagy, Laura R. 1996. Distribution of Bicknell's Thrush in New England and New York. *Wilson Bull.* 108(4): 650–661. Available from http://www.vtecostudies.org/PDF/WB108atwood.pdf.
2. Blodget, Bradford G. 2009. *Birds of Massachusetts A Check-list*. Massachusetts Division of Fisheries & Wildlife. June 2009.

3. DeGraaf, Richard M. and Yamasaki, Mariko. 2001. *New England Wildlife. Habitat, Natural History, and Distribution.* University Press of New England: Hanover. 482 pages.
4. Dunn, Jon L. and Alderfer, Jonathan. 2006. *National Geographic Field Guide to the Birds of North America.* Fifth Edition. National Geographic: Washington, D.C. 503 pages.
5. Forbush, E.H. 1912. *A History of Game Birds, wild-fowl, and Shore Birds of Massachusetts and Adjacent States.* Issued by the Massachusetts State Board of Agriculture. Wright & Potter Printing Company, Boston.
6. Godin, A. J. 1977. *Wild Mammals of New England.* The John Hopkins University Press, Baltimore. 304 pages.
7. Howe, R.H., Jr. and Allen, G.M. 1901. *The Birds of Massachusetts.* Nuttall Ornithological Club and American Ornithologist's Union. Cambridge, MA.
8. Manomet Observatory for Conservation Sciences. 1996. *Field list of Massachusetts birds.* Manomet Observatory Inc. Unpaginated. Jamestown, ND: Northern Prairie Wildlife Research Center Online. http://www.npwrc.usgs.govmass.htm (Version 22MAY98).
9. Mass Audubon. 2010. Interim Report #60: Sandhill Crane. Mass Audubon Blogs. Distraction Displays: Mass Breeding Bird Atlas 2. January 11, 2010. Available from http://massaudubonblogs.typepad.com/massbirdatlas/2010/01/interim-report-60-sandhill-crane.html. Accessed 12/30/2011.
10. MassWildlife. 2004. Living with Wildlife. Wild Turkey in Massachusetts. June 2004. Available from http://www.mass.gov/dfwele/dfw/wildlife/living/pdf/living%20_with_turkeys.pdf.
11. MassWildlife. 2009. Beavers in Massachusetts. Last updated: July 22, 2009. Available from http://www.mass.gov/dfwele/dfw/wildlife/facts/mammals/beaver/beaver_home.htm.
12. MassWildlife. 2009. Fisher in Massachusetts. Last updated: June 15, 2009. Available from http://www.mass.gov/dfwele/dfw/wildlife/living/living_with_fisher.htm.
13. MassWildlife. 2009. State Mammal List. Last Updated: February 20, 2009. Available from http://www.mass.gov/dfwele/dfw/wildlife/facts/mammals/mammal_list.htm.
14. MassWildlife. 2010. Conservation web page. Updated: August 3, 2010. Available from http://www.mass.gov/dfwele/dfw/nhesp/conservation/conservation_home.htm.
15. MassWildlife. 2012. Loons, Lead Sinkers & Jigs. Last Updated February 7, 2012. Available from http://www.mass.gov/dfwele/dfw/recreation/fishing/lead_sinkers_loons.htm.

APPENDIX A: SPECIES EXTIRPATED FROM MASSACHUSETTS 93

16. NHESP (Natural Heritage & Endangered Species Program). 2007. NHESP Fact Sheet: Peregrine Falcon *(Falco peregrinus)*. Commonwealth of Massachusetts Division of Fisheries & Wildlife. Updated December 2007. Available from http://www.mass.gov/dfwele/dfw/nhesp/species_info/nhfacts/falco_peregrinus.pdf.

17. NHESP (Natural Heritage & Endangered Species Program). 2009. NHESP Fact Sheet: Bald Eagle *(Haliaeetus leucocephalus)*. Commonwealth of Massachusetts Division of Fisheries & Wildlife. Updated January 2009. Available from http://www.mass.gov/dfwele/dfw/nhesp/species_info/nhfacts/haliaeetus_leucocephalus.pdf.

Appendix B: List of Bird Species

The following species of birds have been observed in Den Rock Park since 2007. This list was compiled based on my observations from 2007–2012 and those of Kathie Brown (Brown, 2012) from 2010–2012.

	Common Name	Scientific Name
1	Blackbird, Red-winged	*Agelaius phoeniceus* [C, SR]
2	Blackbird, Rusty	*Euphagus carolinus* [R, M]
3	Bluebird, Eastern	*Sialia sialis* [O/C, PR]
4	Bufflehead	*Bucephala albeola* [R, M]
5	Cardinal, Northern	*Cardinalis cardinalis* [C, PR]
6	Catbird, Gray	*Dumetella carolinensis* [O, SR]
7	Chickadee, Black-capped	*Poecile atricapillus* [C, PR]
8	Cormorant, Double-crested	*Phalacrocorax auritus* [R, V]
9	Cowbird, Brown-headed	*Molothrus ater* [O/C, SR]
10	Creeper, Brown	*Certhia americana* [R, SV]
11	Crow, American	*Corvus brachyrhynchos* [C, PR]
12	Dove, Mourning	*Zenaida macroura* [C, PR]
13	Duck, American Black	*Anas rubripes* [R, V]
14	Duck, Ring-necked	*Aythya collaris* [R, M]
15	Duck, Wood	*Aix sponsa* [C, M]
16	Egret, Great	*Ardea alba* [R, M]
17	Falcon, Peregrine	*Falco peregrinus* [R, V]
18	Finch, House	*Carpodacus mexicanus* [R/O, PR]
19	Flicker, Northern	*Colaptes auratus* [C, SR]
20	Flycatcher, Great Crested	*Myiarchus crinitus* [R, M]
21	Goldfinch, American	*Carduelis tristis* [C, PR]
22	Goose, Canada	*Branta canadensis* [C, PR]
23	Grackle, Common	*Quiscalus quiscula* [C, SR]
24	Gull, Herring	*Larus argentatus* [O, PR]
25	Gull, Ring-billed	*Larus delawarensis* [O, PR]

APPENDIX B: LIST OF BIRD SPECIES

	Common Name	**Scientific Name**
26	Hawk, Cooper's	*Accipiter cooperii* [R/O, V]
27	Hawk, Red-tailed	*Buteo jamaicensis* [C, PR]
28	Heron, Great Blue	*Ardea herodias* [C, SR]
29	Heron, Green	*Butorides virescens* [O, SV]
30	Hummingbird, Ruby-throated	*Archilochus colubris* [R, SV]
31	Jay, Blue	*Cyanocitta cristata* [C, PR]
32	Junco, Dark-eyed	*Junco hyemalis* [O/C, WR/M]
33	Kestrel, American	*Falco sparverius* [R, V]
34	Killdeer	*Charadrius vociferus* [R, V]
35	Kingbird, Eastern	*Tyrannus tyrannus* [O/C, SR]
36	Kingfisher, Belted	*Megaceryle alcyon* [O/C, SV]
37	Kinglet, Golden-crowned	*Regulus satrapa* [R, V]
38	Kinglet, Ruby-crowned	*Regulus calendula* [R, V]
39	Mallard	*Anas platyrhynchos* [C, PR]
40	Martin, Purple	*Progne subis* [R, V]
41	Merganser, Hooded	*Lophodytes cucullatus* [O, M]
42	Merlin	*Falco columbarius* [R, V]
43	Mockingbird, Northern	*Mimus polyglottos* [R/O, PR]
44	Night-heron, Black-crowned	*Nycticorax nycticorax* [R/O, SV]
45	Nuthatch, White-breasted	*Sitta carolinensis* [C, PR]
46	Oriole, Baltimore	*Icterus galbula* [O, SR]
47	Osprey	*Pandion haliaetus* [R, V]
48	Ovenbird	*Seiurus aurocapilla* [R, M]
49	Phoebe, Eastern	*Sayornis phoebe* [O/C, SR]
50	Pigeon, Rock	*Columba livia* [R, V]
51	Robin, American	*Turdus migratorius* [C, PR]
52	Sandpiper, Spotted	*Actitis macularius* [R, V]
53	Sparrow, American Tree	*Spizella arborea* [R, W V]
54	Sparrow, Chipping	*Spizella passerina* [O, SR]
55	Sparrow, House	*Passer domesticus* [C, PR]
56	Sparrow, Lincoln's	*Melospiza lincolnii* [R, V]

APPENDIX B: LIST OF BIRD SPECIES

	Common Name	Scientific Name
57	Sparrow, Song	*Melospiza melodia* [C, PR]
58	Sparrow, Swamp	*Melospiza georgiana* [R, V]
59	Sparrow, White-throated	*Zonotrichia albicollis* [R/O, V]
60	Starling, European	*Sturnus vulgaris* [O/C, PR]
61	Swallow, Barn	*Hirundo rustica* [R, M]
62	Swallow, Northern Rough-winged	*Stelgidopteryx serripennis* [R,M]
63	Swallow, Tree	*Tachycineta bicolor* [C, SR]
64	Swift, Chimney	*Chaetura pelagica* [O, SR]
65	Teal, Green-winged	*Anas crecca* [R, M]
66	Titmouse, Tufted	*Baeolophus bicolor* [C, PR]
67	Vulture, Turkey	*Cathartes aura* [O, V]
68	Warbler, Palm	*Dendroica palmarum* [C, M]
69	Warbler, Yellow-rumped	*Dendroica coronata* [C, M]
70	Waxwing, Cedar	*Bombycilla cedrorum* [O, SV/M]
71	Woodpecker, Downy	*Picoides pubescens* [C, PR]
72	Woodpecker, Hairy	*Picoides villosus* [O, PR]
73	Woodpecker, Red-bellied	*Melanerpes carolinus* [O, PR]
74	Wren, Carolina	*Thryothorus ludovicianus* [R/O, PR]
75	Wren, Winter	*Troglodytes hiemalis* [R,V]
76	Yellowthroat, Common	*Geothlypis thrichas* [O, SV]

Notes: Species status is indicated after the scientific name, with frequency of observation provided first followed by residency status.

   C – common
   O – occasional
   R – rare
   SR – summer resident
   SV – summer visitor
   M – migrant
   V – visitor or migrant
   PR – permanent resident
   WR – winter resident
   WV – winter visitor

Bibliography

Adams, Edwin G. 1857. *Historical Discourse in Commemoration of the One Hundredth Anniversary of the Formation of the First Congregational Church in Templeton, Massachusetts.* Crosby, Nichols, and Company: Boston.

American Bird Conservancy. Domestic Cat Predation on Birds and other Wildlife. Available from http://www.abcbirds.org/abcprograms/policy/cats/materials/predation.pdf.

American Sportfishing Association. 2002. The Practical Biological Impacts of Banning Lead Sinkers for Fishing. Position of the American Sportfishing Association. December 4, 2002. Available from http://wdfw.wa.gov/conservation/loons/asa_lead_position.pdf.

Anderson, Rob. 2010. Massachusetts's strange inaction on light pollution. *Boston Globe* editorial. Posted September 28, 2010. Available from http://www.boston.com/bostonglobe/editorial_opinion/blogs/the_angle/2010/09/in_her_column_o.html. Accessed 2/15/2012.

Arcese, Peter, Mark K. Sogge, Amy B. Marr and Michael A. Patten. 2002. Song Sparrow *(Melospiza melodia)*, The Birds of North America Online (A. Poole, Ed.). Ithaca: Cornell Lab of Ornithology; Retrieved from the Birds of North America Online: http://bna.birds.cornell.edu/bna/species/704.

Audubon International. 2006. Wood Duck Conservation Fact Sheet Wildlife and Habitat Management. Available from http://www.auduboninternational.org/PDFs/WHM-%20Wood%20Ducks.pdf.

Bildstein, Keith L. 2001. Raptors as Vermin: A History of Human Attitudes towards Pennsylvania's Birds of Prey. In: *Endangered Species Update* 18 (4): 124–128.

Blodget, Bradford G. 2009. *Birds of Massachusetts A Check-list.* Massachusetts Division of Fisheries & Wildlife. June 2009.

Boston Globe. 1961. Fate of Den Rock Park in Lawrence at Stake. January 15, 1961. Pg. 18.

Brown, Kathie. 2012. "Stirling Bog Species" Kathie's Birds (web log). Available from http://kathiesbirds.blogspot.com/. Accessed May 25, 2012.

Butcher, Gregory S., and Daniel K. Niven. 2007. Combining Data from the Christmas Bird Count and the Breeding Bird Survey to Determine the Continental Status and Trends of North America Birds. (a National Audubon Society report). June 14, 2007.

Cabe, Paul R. 1993. European Starling *(Sturnus vulgaris)*, The Birds of North America Online (A. Poole, Ed.). Ithaca: Cornell Lab of Ornithology; Retrieved from the Birds of North America Online: http://bna.birds.cornell.edu/bna/species/048.

Carovillano, Jeffrey R. 2002. Adaptation and Resistance. An Analysis of Native American Activity at Den Rock during the Contact Period, ca. 1625 – 1675. M.A. Thesis. University of Massachusetts Boston.

Carson, Rachel. 1962. *Silent Spring.* Houghton Mifflin Company: Boston. 368 pages.

Chase, Jameson F., and Alexander Cruz. 1998. Range of the Brown-headed Cowbird in Colorado: past and present. *Great Basin Naturalist* 58 (3): 245–249.

Choate, E.A. 1985. *The dictionary of American bird names.* Harvard Common Press, Boston, Massachusetts.

City of Lawrence and Groundwork Lawrence (undated). Den Rock Park Trail Guide.

City of Lowell. 2002. Comprehensive Master Plan Existing Conditions Report. City of Lowell, Massachusetts. Prepared by the City of Lowell Division of Planning and Development and the City of Lowell Planning Board. February 2002. Available from http://www.lowellma.gov/depts/dpd/master_plan/exist_cond/.

Cummings, John L. and Michael L. Avery. 2003. An overview of current blackbird research in the southern rice growing region of the United States. *USDA National Wildlife Research Center - Staff Publications.* Paper 207.

Daily Boston Globe. 1935. Work on Park at Lawrence Recalls Den Rock Stories. *Special Dispatch to the Globe.* July 7, 1935. Pg. A4.

Davis, Jr., W. E. and J. A. Kushlan. 1994. Green Heron *(Butorides virescens)*, The Birds of North America Online (A. Poole, Ed.). Ithaca: Cornell Lab of Ornithology; Retrieved from the Birds of North America Online: http://bna.birds.cornell.edu/bna/species/129.

DeGraaf, Richard M. and Mariko Yamasaki. 2001. *New England Wildlife. Habitat, Natural History, and Distribution.* University Press of New England: Hanover. 482 pages.

Dolbeer, R.A., D.F. Mott, and J.L. Belant. 1997. Blackbirds and starlings killed at winter roosts from PA-14 applications, 1974–1992: implications for regional population management. *Proc. Eastern Wildlife Damage Management Conference.* 7:77–86. Seventh Eastern Wildlife Damage Management Conference, 1995. University of Nebraska – Lincoln.

Dorgan, Maurice, B. 1918. *Lawrence, Yesterday and Today (1845–1918). A Concise History of Lawrence, Massachusetts – Her Industries and Institutions; Municipal Statistics and a Variety of Information Concerning the City.* Press of Dick & Trumpold.

Drilling, Nancy, Rodger Titman and Frank Mckinney. 2002. Mallard (*Anas platyrhynchos*), The Birds of North America Online (A. Poole, Ed.). Ithaca: Cornell Lab of Ornithology; Retrieved from the Birds of North America Online: http://bna.birds.cornell.edu/bna/species/658.

Ehrlich, Paul R., David S. Dobkin, and Darryl Wheye. 1988. *The Birder's Handbook. A Field Guide to the Natural History of North American Birds.* Simon & Schuster, Inc.: New York. 785 pages.

Elwell, Alice. 2012. Rare visitor may hint at climate shift. *The Boston Globe.* Globe West. January 26, 2012. p. 1.

Essex National Heritage Area. 2011. Lawrence History from the Essex National Heritage Area's web page Lawrence History Center: Immigrant City Archives and Museum. Available from http://www.essexheritage.org/sites/immigrant_city.shtml.

Executive Office of Environmental Affairs. 2003. Shawsheen River. Watershed Assessment Report 2002–2007. July 2003. http://www.mass.gov/Eoeea/docs/eea/water/assess_rpt_shawsheen_2002.pdf.

Evans, William R., Yukio Akashi, Naomi S. Altman, and Albert M. Manville, II. 2007. Response of night-migrating songbirds in cloud to colored and flashing light, *North American Birds* 60 (4): 476–488.

Fisher Museum Harvard Forest. 2008. Landscape History of Central New England. Available from http://harvardforest.fas.harvard.edu/museum/landscape.html#height.

Foote, Jennifer R., Daniel J. Mennill, Laurene M. Ratcliffe and Susan M. Smith. 2010. Black-capped Chickadee *(Poecile atricapillus)*, The Birds of North America Online (A. Poole, Ed.). Ithaca: Cornell Lab of Ornithology; Retrieved from the Birds of North America Online: http://bna.birds.cornell.edu/bna/species/039.

Forbush, E.H. 1912. *A History of the Game Birds, wild-fowl, and Shore Birds of Massachusetts and Adjacent States.* Issued by the Massachusetts State Board of Agriculture. Wright & Potter Printing Company, Boston.

Foster, D.R., B.M. Donahue, D.B. Kittredge, K.F. Lambert, M.L. Hunter, B.R. Hall, L.C. Irland, R.J. Lilieholm, D.A. Orwig, A.W. D'Amato, E.A. Colburn, J.R. Thompson, J.N. Levitt, A.M. Ellison, W.S. Keeton, J.D. Aber, C.V. Cogbill, C.T. Driscoll, T.J. Fahey, and C.M. Hart. 2010. *Wildlands and Woodlands: A Vision for the New England Landscape.* Harvard Forest, dist. by Harvard University Press, Cambridge, Massachusetts. 36pp.

Frumhoff, P.C., J.J. McCarthy, J.M. Melillo, S.C. Moser, and D.J. Wuebbles. 2007. Confronting Climate Change in the U.S. Northeast: Science, Impacts, and Solutions. Synthesis report of the Northeast Climate Impacts Assessment (NECIA). Cambridge, MA: Union of Concerned Scientists (UCS).

Geist, Valerius. 1996. *Buffalo Nation.* History and Legend of the North American Bison. Voyageur Press: Stillwater, MN. 144 pages.

Gowaty, Patricia Adair and Jonathan H. Plissner. 1998. Eastern Bluebird *(Sialia sialis)*, The Birds of North America Online (A. Poole, Ed.). Ithaca: Cornell Lab of Ornithology; Retrieved from the Birds of North America Online: http://bna.birds.cornell.edu/bna/species/381.

Griscom, L. and D.E. Snyder. 1955. *The birds of Massachusetts – An annotated and revised check list.* Salem, Mass.: Peabody Museum. 295 pp.

Grubb, Jr., T. C. and V. V. Pravosudov. 2008. White-breasted Nuthatch *(Sitta carolinensis)*, The Birds of North America Online (A. Poole, Ed.). Ithaca: Cornell Lab of Ornithology; Retrieved from the Birds of North America Online: http://bna.birds.cornell.edu/bna/species/054.

Grubb, Jr, T. C. and V. V. Pravasudov. 1994. Tufted Titmouse *(Baeolophus bicolor)*, The Birds of North America Online (A. Poole, Ed.). Ithaca: Cornell Lab of Ornithology; Retrieved from the Birds of North America Online: http://bna.birds.cornell.edu/bna/species/086.

Guarino, Joseph, L. 1984. Current status of research on the blackbird-sunflower problem in North Dakota. *Proceedings of the Eleventh Vertebrate Pest Conference.* University of Nebraska – Lincoln.

Halkin, Sylvia L. and Susan U. Linville. 1999. Northern Cardinal *(Cardinalis cardinalis)*, The Birds of North America Online (A. Poole, Ed.). Ithaca: Cornell Lab of Ornithology; Retrieved from the Birds of North America Online: http://bna.birds.cornell.edu/bna/species/440.

Hall, C. Scott and Stephen W. Kress. 2008. Diet of nestling Black-crowned Night-herons in a mixed species colony: implications for tern conservation. *The Wilson Journal of Ornithology* 120(3): 637–640.

Harrison, Hal H. 1975. *A Field Guide to Birds' Nests.* United States East of the Mississippi River. Houghton Mifflin Company: Boston. 257 pages.

Heinrich, Bernd. 2004. *The Geese of Beaver Bog.* HarperCollins Publishers: New York. 217 pages.

Hepp, Gary R. and Frank C. Bellrose. 1995. Wood Duck *(Aix sponsa)*, The Birds of North America Online (A. Poole, Ed.). Ithaca: Cornell Lab of Ornithology; Retrieved from the Birds of North America Online: http://bna.birds.cornell.edu/bna/species/169.

Heusmann, H.W. 1974. Mallard – Black Duck Relationships in the Northeast. *Wildl. Soc. Bull.* 2(4): 171–177.

Heusmann, H.W. and Richard Burrell. 1984. Park waterfowl populations in Massachusetts. *J. Field Ornithol.* 55 (1): 89–96.

Hothem, Roger L., Brianne E. Brussee and William E. Davis, Jr. 2010. Black-crowned Night-Heron *(Nycticorax nycticorax)*, The Birds of North America Online (A. Poole, Ed.). Ithaca: Cornell Lab of Ornithology; Retrieved from the Birds of North America Online: http://bna.birds.cornell.edu/bna/species/074.

Howe, R.H., Jr. and G.M. Allen. 1901. *The Birds of Massachusetts.* Nuttall Ornithological Club and American Ornithologist's Union. Cambridge, MA.

IPCC (Intergovernmental Panel on Climate Change). 2007. Summary for Policymakers. In: Climate Change 2007: The Physical Science Basis. Contribution of Working Group I to the Fourth Assessment Report of the Intergovernmental Panel on Climate Change [Solomon, S., D. Qin, M. Manning, Z. Chen, M. Marquis, K.B. Averyt, M.Tignor and H.L. Miller (eds.)]. Cambridge University Press, Cambridge, UK and New York, NY, USA.

Jackson, Jerome A. and Henri R. Ouellet. 2002. Downy Woodpecker *(Picoides pubescens)*, The Birds of North America Online (A. Poole, Ed.). Ithaca: Cornell Lab of Ornithology; Retrieved from the Birds of North America Online: http://bna.birds.cornell.edu/bna/species/613.

Jackson, Jerome A., Henri R. Ouellet and Bette J. Jackson. 2002. Hairy Woodpecker *(Picoides villosus)*, The Birds of North America Online (A. Poole, Ed.). Ithaca: Cornell Lab of Ornithology; Retrieved from the Birds of North America Online: http://bna.birds.cornell.edu/bna/species/702.

Johnson, W.C. and C.S. Adkisson. 1986. Airlifting the oaks. *Natural History* 95 (10): 40–47.

Jonsson, Patrick. 2010. Bye Bye Blackbird: USDA acknowledges a hand in one mass bird death. *The Christian Science Monitor.* January 20, 2010.

Kelly, Jeffrey F., Eli S. Bridge and Michael J. Hamas. 2009. Belted Kingfisher *(Megaceryle alcyon)*, The Birds of North America Online (A. Poole, Ed.). Ithaca: Cornell Lab of Ornithology; Retrieved from the Birds of North America Online: http://bna.birds.cornell.edu/bna/species/084.

Klimstra, Jon D. and Paul I. Padding. 2012. Harvest distribution and derivation of Atlantic Flyway Canada Geese. *Journal of Fish and Wildlife Management* 3 (1): 43–55.

LeBlanc, Steve. 2010. Report Finds Forest Cover Declining in New England. *Associated Press.* Reprinted in the *Brattleboro Reformer.* May 20.

Li, J., T. Zhu, F. Wang, X.H. Qiu, and W.L. Lin. 2006. Observation of organochlorine pesticides in the air of the Mt. Everest region. *Ecotoxicology and Environmental Safety* 63 (1): 33–41.

Lockwood, Julie L., Martha F. Hoopes, and Michael P. Marchetti. 2007. *Invasion Ecology.* Blackwell Publishing Ltd. Malden, MA. 304 pages.

Lowe, S., M. Browne, S. Boudjelas, M. De Poorter, 2000. 100 of the World's Worst Invasive Alien Species: A selection from the Global Invasive Species Database. Published by The Invasive Species Specialist Group (ISSG) a specialist group of the Species Survival Commission (SSC) of the World Conservation Union (IUCN), 12 pp. Updated November 2004.

Lowther, Peter E. 1993. Brown-headed Cowbird *(Molothrus ater),* The Birds of North America Online (A. Poole, Ed.). Ithaca: Cornell Lab of Ornithology; Retrieved from the Birds of North America Online: http://bna.birds.cornell.edu/bna/species/047.

BIBLIOGRAPHY

Lowther, Peter E. and Calvin L. Cink. 2006. House Sparrow *(Passer domesticus)*, The Birds of North America Online (A. Poole, Ed.). Ithaca: Cornell Lab of Ornithology; Retrieved from the Birds of North America Online: http://bna.birds.cornell.edu/bna/species/012.

Malecki, Richard A., Bruce D.J. Batt, and Susan E. Sheaffer. 2001. Spatial and temporal distribution of Atlantic Population Canada Geese. *The Journal of Wildlife Management* 65 (2): 242–247.

Mass Audubon. 2003. Massachusetts Breeding Bird Atlas 1. Available at http://www.massaudubon.org/birdatlas/bba1/index.php.

Mass Audubon. 2009. Interim Reports [available for various species]. Mass Audubon Blogs. Breeding Bird Atlas 2. Available from http://massaudubonblogs.typepad.com/massbirdatlas/. Accessed August 2011.

Mass Audubon. 2009. Losing Ground. Beyond the Footprint. Patterns of Development and their Impact on the Nature of Massachusetts. Fourth edition. May 2009.

Mass Audubon. 2011. A History of Grassland Birds in the Northeast from Mass Audubon's Grassland Birds web page. Available from http://www.massaudubon.org/Birds_and_Birding/grassland/#history.

Mass Audubon. 2011. Living with Wildlife: Bird Species: Great Blue Heron. Available from http://www.massaudubon.org/Nature_Connection/wildlife/index.php?subject=Birds:%20Species&id=49. Accessed 7/8/2011.

Mass Audubon. 2011. State of the Birds. Available from http://www.massaudubon.org/StateoftheBirds/.

Mass Audubon. 2012. Lights Out web page. Available from http://www.massaudubon.org/lightsout/. Accessed 2/15/2012.

MassWildlife. 2006. Commonwealth of Massachusetts Comprehensive Wildlife Conservation Strategy. Available from http://www.wildlifeactionplans.org/massachusetts.html.

MassWildlife. 2007. Hunting of Crows. Available from http://www.mass.gov/dfwele/dfw/regulations/plain_language/hunting_crows.htm.
MassWildlife. 2009. Beavers in Massachusetts. Available from http://www.mass.gov/dfwele/dfw/wildlife/facts/mammals/beaver/beaver_home.htm.
MassWildlife. 2009. Waterfowl Studies. Available from http://www.mass.gov/dfwele/dfw/wildlife/facts/birds/waterfowl/waterfowl_home.htm. 2/05/09.
MassWildlife. 2010. Migratory Bird Regulations for 2011–12 Season. Available from http://www.mass.gov/dfwele/dfw/regulations/abstracts/migratory_bird_regs.pdf.
MassWildlife. 2010. Massachusetts Fish & Wildlife Guide to Hunting, Fishing and Trapping. Available from http://www.mass.gov/dfwele/dfw/dfwpdf/dfwab01.pdf.
MassWildlife. 2012. Loons, Lead Sinkers & Jigs. Available from http://www.mass.gov/dfwele/dfw/recreation/fishing/lead_sinkers_loons.htm. Last updated February 7, 2012.
MassWildlife. 2013. Canada Geese in Massachusetts. Available from http://www.mass.gov/dfwele/dfw/wildlife/living/living_with_geese.htm. Updated 1/03/2013.
McLean, Robert G. 2004. West Nile Virus: Impact on Crow Populations in the United States. *Proc. 21st Vertebr. Pest Conf.* (R M. Timm and W. P. Gorenzel, Eds.) Published at Univ. of Calif, Davis. 2004. Pp. 180–184.
McMillan, Jean. 1995. Mall Proposed for Den Rock. *The Eagle Tribune.* January 31, 1995. p. 1.
Mecklenburg Audubon Society. Birds We Love to Hate: Grackles. Mecklenburg Audubon Society. North Carolina. Available from http://meckbirds.org/idbehavior/pdfs/grackles.pdf.
Michigan Department of Natural Resources. 2012. Kirtland's Warbler *(Dendroica kirtlandii).* Available from http://www.michigan.gov/dnr/0,1607,7-153-10370_12145_12202-32591--,00.html.
Miller, Mark W. 2006. Apparent effects of light pollution on singing behavior of American Robins. *The Condor* 108 (1): 130–139.

Mirick, Peter G. 2011. White Nose: Disaster for the Bats. *Massachusetts Wildlife* (3): 14–28.

Mofford, Juliet Haines. 1980. *AVIS – A History of Conservation*. Andover Village Improvement Society, Andover, MA. 238 pages.

Morse, Albert P. 1912. *A Pocket List of the Birds of Eastern Massachusetts with Especial Reference to Essex County*. Peabody Academy of Science: Salem, Mass.

Mostello, C.S. 2007. Roseate Tern *(Sterna dougallii)*. Natural Heritage & Endangered Species Program fact sheet. Commonwealth of Massachusetts Division of Fisheries & Wildlife. Available from http://www.mass.gov/dfwele/dfw/nhesp/species_info/nhfacts/roseate_tern.pdf.

Mott, D.F. 1984. Research on winter roosting blackbirds and starlings in the southeastern United States. *Proceedings Eleventh Vertebrate Pest Conference* (D.O. Clark, Ed.). Printed at Univ. of California, Davis, Calif. Pp. 183–187.

Mowbray, Thomas B., Craig R. Ely, James S. Sedinger and Robert E. Trost. 2002. Canada Goose *(Branta canadensis)*, The Birds of North America Online (A. Poole, Ed.). Ithaca: Cornell Lab of Ornithology; Retrieved from the Birds of North America Online: http://bna.birds.cornell.edu/bna/species/682.

Murphy, Michael T. 1996. Eastern Kingbird *(Tyrannus tyrannus)*, The Birds of North America Online (A. Poole, Ed.). Ithaca: Cornell Lab of Ornithology; Retrieved from the Birds of North America Online: http://bna.birds.cornell.edu/bna/species/253.

NELPAG (New England Light Pollution Advisory Group). 2011. Massachusetts Bill S.1651. Available from http://nelpag.harvee.org/S_1651. Last edited 6-23-2011.

The New York Times. 1877. American Acclimatization Society. November 15, 1877.

Otis, David L., John H. Schulz, David Miller, R. E. Mirarchi and T. S. Baskett. 2008. Mourning Dove *(Zenaida macroura)*, The Birds of North America Online (A. Poole, Ed.). Ithaca: Cornell Lab of Ornithology; Retrieved from the Birds of North America Online: http://bna.birds.cornell.edu/bna/species/117.

Patterson, Bruce M. 2006. The Marsh at Den Rock Park. Lawrence, Massachusetts. Botanical Resource Inventory & Management Recommendations. November.

Payne, Robert B. 1977. The ecology of brood parasitism in birds. *Annual Review of Ecology and Systematics* 8: 1–28.

Peer, Brian D. and Eric K. Bollinger. 1998. Rejection of Cowbird Eggs by Mourning Doves: A Manifestation of Nest Usurpation? *The Auk* 115(4): 1057–1062.

Peer, Brian D. and Eric K. Bollinger. 1997. Common Grackle *(Quiscalus quiscula)*, The Birds of North America Online (A. Poole, Ed.). Ithaca: Cornell Lab of Ornithology; Retrieved from the Birds of North America Online: http://bna.birds.cornell.edu/bna/species/271.

Phillips, John B., Rachel Muheim, and Paulo E. Jorge. 2010. A behavioral perspective on the biophysics of the light-dependent magnetic compass: a link between directional and spatial perception? *The Journal of Experimental Biology* 213: 3247–3255.

Preston, C. R. and R. D. Beane. 2009. Red-tailed Hawk *(Buteo jamaicensis)*, The Birds of North America Online (A. Poole, Ed.). Ithaca: Cornell Lab of Ornithology; Retrieved from the Birds of North America Online: http://bna.birds.cornell.edu/bna/species/052.

Primack, Daniel, Carolyn Imbres, Richard B. Primack, Abraham J. Miller-Rushing, Peter Del Tredici. 2004. Herbarium specimens demonstrate earlier flowering times in response to warming in Boston. *American Journal of Botany* 91:1260–1264.

Robinson, R. A., G. M. Siriwardena, and H.Q.P. Crick. 2006. Size and trends of the House Sparrow Passer domesticus population in Great Britain. *Ibis* 147: 552–562.

Robinson, R. A., G. M. Siriwardena, and H.Q.P. Crick. 2006. S31-1 The population decline of the starling, *Sturnus vulgaris*, in Great Britain: patterns and causes. *Acta Zoologica Sinica* 52 (Supplement): 550–553.

Robinson, Scott K. and David S. Wilcove. 1994. Forest fragmentation in the temperate zone and its effects on migratory songbirds. *Bird Conservation International* 4: 233–249.

Root, Oscar M. 1957–58. *The Birds of the Andover Region*. Reprinted from Bulletin of the Mass. Audubon Society. Vol. XLI. No. 9; Vol XLII, Nos. 1, 2,3.

The Royal Society for the Protection of Birds. 2009. Birds of Conservation Concern 3: The Population Status of Birds in the United Kingdom, Channel Islands, and the Isle of Man. Available from http://www.rspb.org.uk/wildlife/birdguide/status_explained.aspx.

Sallabanks, Rex and Frances C. James. 1999. American Robin *(Turdus migratorius)*, The Birds of North America Online (A. Poole, Ed.). Ithaca: Cornell Lab of Ornithology; Retrieved from the Birds of North America Online: http://bna.birds.cornell.edu/bna/species/462.

Sauer, J. R., J. E. Hines, J. E. Fallon, K. L. Pardieck, D. J. Ziolkowski, Jr., and W. A. Link. 2011. The North American Breeding Bird Survey, Results and Analysis 1966–2009. Version 3.23.2011 USGS Patuxent Wildlife Research Center, Laurel, MD.

Schulz, J. H., P. I. Padding, and J. J. Millspaugh. 2006. Will mourning dove crippling rates increase with nontoxic-shot regulations? *Wildlife Society Bulletin* 34 (3):861–865.

Secretary of the Commonwealth Citizen Information Service. State Symbols. Available from http://www.sec.state.ma.us/cis/cismaf/mf1a.htm.

Shackelford, Clifford E., Raymond E. Brown and Richard N. Conner. 2000. Red-bellied Woodpecker *(Melanerpes carolinus)*, The Birds of North America Online (A. Poole, Ed.). Ithaca: Cornell Lab of Ornithology; Retrieved from the Birds of North America Online: http://bna.birds.cornell.edu/bna/species/500.

Stockholm Convention. 2012. DDT Register Pursuant to Paragraph 1 of Part II of Annex B of the Stockholm Convention. Available from http://chm.pops.int/Implementation/Exemptions/AcceptablePurposesDDT/tabid/456/Default.aspx.

Stokes, Donald. 1979. *A Guide to Bird Behavior. Volume I*. Little, Brown and Company: Boston. 336 pages.

Stokes, Donald and Lillian. 1983. *A Guide to Bird Behavior. Volume II. In the Wild and at Your Feeder.* Stokes Nature Guides. Little, Brown and Company: Boston. 334 pages.

Stokes, Donald and Lillian. 1989. *A Guide to Bird Behavior. Volume III.* Little, Brown and Company: Boston. 397 pages.

Stokes, Donald and Lillian. 1996. *Field Guide to Birds. Eastern Region.* Little, Brown and Company: Boston. 471 pages.

Streater, Scott and *Environmental Health News.* 2009. Wild meat raises lead exposure. *Scientific American.* September 28, 2009. Available online from http://www.scientificamerican.com.

Summers-Smith, J.D. 2003. The decline of the House Sparrow: a review. *British Birds* 96: 439–446.

Tallamy, Douglas W. 2007. *Bringing Nature Home. How You Can Sustain Wildlife with Native Plants.* Timber Press: Portland. 358 pages.

Tarvin, Keith A. and Glen E. Woolfenden. 1999. Blue Jay *(Cyanocitta cristata)*, The Birds of North America Online (A. Poole, Ed.). Ithaca: Cornell Lab of Ornithology; Retrieved from the Birds of North America Online: http://bna.birds.cornell.edu/bna/species/469.

Terborgh, John. 1989. *Where Have All the Birds Gone?* Princeton University Press: Princeton, NJ. 207 pages.

UMass Extension, Center for Agriculture. 2008. Starling Damage Assessment website. Last updated February 5, 2008. Available from http://www.extension.org/pages/11410/starling-damage-assessment.

USDA (United States Department of Agriculture) Forest Service. 2006. The Forest Resources of Massachusetts, 2005. A USDA Forest Inventory & Analysis Update. April 25.

USDA (United States Department of Agriculture) Animal and Plant Health Inspection Service (APHIS) Wildlife Services. 2009. Table G. Animals Taken by Component/Method Type and Fate by Wildlife Services - FY 2009. 745 pages. Available from http://www.aphis.usda.gov/wildlife_damage/prog_data/2009_prog_data/PDR_G_FY09/Basic_Tables_PDR_G/Table_G_FY2009_Long_Method_Featured.pdf.

USDA (United States Department of Agriculture) Animal and Plant Health Inspection Service (APHIS) Wildlife Services. 2009. Table G-2. Animals Euthanized or Killed by Wildlife Services - FY 2009. 70 pages. Available from http://www.aphis.usda.gov/wildlife_damage/prog_data/2009_prog_data/PDR_G_FY09/Basic_Tables_PDR_G/Table_G-2_FY2009_Euth-Killed.pdf.

USDA (United States Department of Agriculture) Animal and Plant Health Inspection Service (APHIS) Wildlife Services. 2010. Table G. Animals Taken by Component/Method Type and Fate by Wildlife Services - FY 2010. 801 pages. Available from http://www.aphis.usda.gov/wildlife_damage/prog_data/2010_prog_data/PDR_G/Basic_Tables_PDR_G/Table_G_Long_Method_Featured.pdf.

USDA (United States Department of Agriculture) Animal and Plant Health Inspection Service (APHIS) Wildlife Services. 2010. Table G. Animals Taken by Wildlife Services – FY 2010. 38 pages. Available from http://www.aphis.usda.gov/wildlife_damage/prog_data/2010_prog_data/PDR_G/Basic_Tables_PDR_G/Table%20G_ShortReport.pdf.

USDA (United States Department of Agriculture) Animal and Plant Health Inspection Service (APHIS) Wildlife Services. 2011. Table G. Animals Taken by Component/Method Type and Fate by Wildlife Services - FY 2011. 889 pages. Available from http://www.aphis.usda.gov/wildlife_damage/prog_data/2011_prog_data/PDR_G/Basic_Tables_PDR_G/Table_G_Long_Method_Featured.pdf.

USDA (United States Department of Agriculture) Animal and Plant Health Inspection Service (APHIS) Wildlife Services. 2011. Table G. Animals Taken by Wildlife Services – FY 2011. 36 pages. Available from http://www.aphis.usda.gov/wildlife_damage/prog_data/2011_prog_data/PDR_G/Basic_Tables_PDR_G/Table%20G_ShortReport.pdf.

U.S. EPA (United States Environmental Protection Agency). 2010. Climate Change Indicators in the United States. Available from http://www.epa.gov/climatechange/indicators/pdfs/ClimateIndicators_full.pdf.

USFS (U.S. Forest Service). 2006. U.S. Forest Service. *Four Threats – Quick Facts*. Last updated October 30, 2006. Available from http://www.fs.fed.us/projects/four-threats/facts/open-space.shtml.

USFWS (U.S. Fish and Wildlife Service). 1999. Let's get the lead out! October 1999. Available from http://www.fws.gov/contaminants/Documents/leadpoisoning2.pdf.

USFWS (U.S. Fish and Wildlife Service). 2000. Pesticides and Birds. March 2000. Available from http://library.fws.gov/pubs/mbd_pesticides-3-00.pdf.

USFWS (U.S. Fish and Wildlife Service). 2000. Service continues to expand non-toxic shot options as study shows ban on lead shot saves millions of waterfowl. October 25. 00-177. Available from http://www.fws.gov/pacific/news/2000/2000-177.htm.

USFWS (U.S. Fish and Wildlife Service). 2002. Migratory Bird Mortality. Available from http://www.fws.gov/birds/mortality-fact-sheet.pdf.

USFWS (U.S. Fish and Wildlife Service). 2005. Definitely a Bird of a Different Color. *On the Wild Side* (e-newsletter for the Chesapeake Bay Field Office). Summer 2005. Available from http://www.fws.gov/chesapeakebay/newsletter/Summer05/Wood%20ducks/Wood%20ducks.htm.

USFWS (U.S. Fish and Wildlife Service). 2010. Migratory Bird Permits; Removal of Rusty Blackbird and Tamaulipas (Mexican) Crow from the Depredation Order for Blackbirds, Cowbirds, Grackles, Crows, and Magpies, and other Changes to the Order. *Federal Register.* December 2, 2010.

Veit, R. and W.R. Petersen. 1993. *Birds of Massachusetts.* Lincoln: Massachusetts Audubon Society. 514 pages.

Vennesland, Ross G. and Robert W. Butler. 2011. Great Blue Heron *(Ardea herodias),* The Birds of North America Online (A. Poole, Ed.). Ithaca: Cornell Lab of Ornithology; Retrieved from the Birds of North America Online: http://bna.birds.cornell.edu/bna/species/025.

Verbeek, N. A. and C. Caffrey. 2002. American Crow *(Corvus brachyrhynchos)*, The Birds of North America Online (A. Poole, Ed.). Ithaca: Cornell Lab of Ornithology; Retrieved from the Birds of North America Online: http://bna.birds.cornell.edu/bna/species/647.

Vogler, Mark E. 2007. Den Rock Park Protected Forever. New Zoning Will Preserve Land. *The Eagle Tribune.* August 10, 2007. Pp. 1, 10.

Waters, Wilson and Henry Spaulding Perham,. 1917. *History of Chelmsford, Massachusetts.* Printed for the town by Courier-Citizen Company: Lowell, Massachusetts.

Weeks Jr., Harmon P. 2011. Eastern Phoebe *(Sayornis phoebe)*, The Birds of North America Online (A. Poole, Ed.). Ithaca: Cornell Lab of Ornithology; Retrieved from the Birds of North America Online: http://bna.birds.cornell.edu/bna/species/094.

Wefer, Michael A.; Joseph W. Lee, and William G. Minser. 1993. Use Patterns of Nuisance Black-crowned Night Herons on a Hydroelectric Dam in Eastern Tennessee. *Sixth Eastern Wildlife Damage Control Conference* (1993). Paper 36.

Wetlands Preservation, Inc. 1998. Wetland Replacement Program "Stirling Woods". Stirling Street Expansion, Andover, Massachusetts. Prepared for FPF Corporation. December 14.

Wetlands Preservation, Inc. 1998. Wildlife Habitat Evaluation of Stirling Woods. Stirling Street Expansion, Andover, Massachusetts. Prepared for FPF Corporation. Revised February 2.

Wiebe, Karen L. and William S. Moore. 2008. Northern Flicker *(Colaptes auratus)*, The Birds of North America Online (A. Poole, Ed.). Ithaca: Cornell Lab of Ornithology; Retrieved from the Birds of North America Online: http://bna.birds.cornell.edu/bna/species/166a.

Wilson, J. M. 2001. Beavers in Connecticut: Their natural history and management. Connecticut Department of Environmental Protection, Wildlife Division. Hartford, CT. 18 pp.

Wiltschko, Roswitha, Katrin Stapput, Peter Thalau and Wolfgang Wiltschko. 2010. Directional orientation of birds by the magnetic field under different light conditions. *J. R. Soc. Interface* 6 April 2010 vol. 7 no. Suppl 2 S163-S177.

Wimberly, Ryan L., Tony A. Slowik, H. Jeffrey Homan, and Linda B. Penry, 2004. Using Geographic Information Systems (GIS) software to predict blackbird nesting locations in North Dakota. *Proc. 21st Vertebr. Pest Conf.* Published at Univ. of Calif., Davis. Pp. 83-86.

Winkler, David W., Kelly K. Hallinger, Daniel R. Ardia, R. J. Robertson, B. J. Stutchbury and R. R. Cohen. 2011. Tree Swallow *(Tachycineta bicolor)*, The Birds of North America Online (A. Poole, Ed.). Ithaca: Cornell Lab of Ornithology; Retrieved from the Birds of North America Online: http://bna.birds.cornell.edu/bna/species/011.

Wurster, Doris H., Charles F. Wurster Jr., and Walter N. Strickland. 1965. Bird Mortality Following DDT Spray for Dutch Elm Disease. *Ecology* 46 (4): 488-499.

Yasukawa, Ken and William A. Searcy. 1995. Red-winged Blackbird *(Agelaius phoeniceus)*, The Birds of North America Online (A. Poole, Ed.). Ithaca: Cornell Lab of Ornithology; Retrieved from the Birds of North America Online: http://bna.birds.cornell.edu/bna/species/184.

Acknowledgments

Many people helped to make this guide possible. I would like to thank David Larson, the director of Mass Audubon's Birder's Certificate Program, and all the other excellent instructors from the program from whom I've learned much about birds. I am grateful to Kathie Brown of Kathie's Birds for sharing her impressive list of bird species for Den Rock's Beaver Pond. Many thanks to Ed Bell from the Massachusetts Historical Commission for providing me with insight on the history of Den Rock and for writing a summary of the known archaeology and native history of the park for inclusion in this guide. In addition, I am grateful to Bonnie Sousa of the Robert S. Peabody Museum of Archaeology for showing me artifacts from Den Rock Park from the museum's collections and for answering my many questions. The photographs on pages 5 to 7 are courtesy of the Robert S. Peabody Museum of Archaeology. I appreciate the assistance and information provided by Louise Sandberg of the Lawrence Public Library, Dianne Roderick of the Town of Andover Conservation Division, Andrew Wall of the City of Lawrence, Rose Gonzalez of Groundwork Lawrence, Susan Lawrence and Randy Dettmers of the U.S. Fish and Wildlife Service, and H. Heusmann and Andrew Vitz of the Massachusetts Division of Fisheries and Wildlife. I would like to thank my husband, Steve Matava, for his patience and support, and for accompanying me on numerous trips to Den Rock Park in search of birds. Finally, I would like to thank the various people over the years who served as advocates for the park—without their efforts the park would not exist today.

Den Rock

CPSIA information can be obtained at www.ICGtesting.com
Printed in the USA
BVOW10234031O113

312128BV00002B/4/P